Forbidden

The Female Pope

Two years, five months, and four days, 855–858

JUDITH J. SLATER

This is a work of fiction. Names, characters, places, events, and incidents are either the products of the authors' imagination or used in a fictitious manner. Any resemblance to actual persons, living or dead, or actual events, is purely coincidental.

Published by
Judith Slater
TAMARAC, FL

ISBN: 978-0-578-60386-5

Copyright © 2019 by Judith J. Slater

All rights reserved. No part of this book may be reproduced or used in any form or by any means, electronic, digital, or mechanical, including photocopying, scanning, recording, or by any information storage and retrieval system, without permission in writing from the publisher.

Cover and Interior design
Gary A. Rosenberg • www.thebookcouple.com

Printed in the United States of America

Prologue

The One and Only Female Pope in the Vatican
Translated from the Yiddish by Miriam Hoffman
(with her permission)

Two great rebbes, Reb Motele Tchernobiler of the Tchernobiler dynasty in the city of Tchernobil in the Ukraine, and Reb Yisroeltche Rizhiner stemming from the city of Rizhin, conducted an exchange of dialogues and ideas. Each one of them had in mind to outdo the other in storytelling, and so Reb Yisroeltche Rizhiner began spinning his tale in the Chassidic tradition:

> One day, a very distressed khosid (pious Jew) came rushing into the rebbe's house with a plea: "Rebbe! only your blessing can save my wife from her very difficult labor."
>
> The rebbe, realizing that the man was distraught, comforted him: "Not only will I bless you, but I will tell you a story. This is a true story about a very bright young woman who lived in Rome and was steeped in the Catholic lore but couldn't attend the Catholic Seminary due to the fact that she was a woman.
>
> "So, she decided to disguise herself as a young man and attend the Catholic Academy of Rome. As an excellent and valued

student of religion, she made a name for herself and in time was promoted to the priesthood, then bishop, until she was appointed Cardinal. Of course, no one suspected that she was a woman; the secret remained with her.

"As time passed, the Pope died and the Vatican was about to select a new Pope in Rome. A search began and they came upon this extraordinary Cardinal, not suspecting that she was a woman, and proclaimed her Pope over all Catholics.

"As it is well known, the priests were always inclined to transgress, to sin on the side, and indeed the new Pope, during the nights, frequented the streets and alleys of Rome and no one suspected that she was the Pope of Rome. In the midst of her orgies, the female Pope discovered that she was with child, and due to the fact that the Pope wore wide garments, no one knew she was in the family way.

"It all came to a head during the Christian holiday of Easter, when Rome was beleaguered with an enormous crowd of pilgrims who came from all over the world to partake in the Easter holiday. It is said that every year at the same time, a great podium is erected on the balcony of the Vatican, the very place where Popes deliver their papal sermons.

"And the Pope appeared facing the big crowd, but in the midst of her sermon she felt her labor pains coming on and before you knew it, she gave birth to a baby boy. The entire Vatican was thunderstruck, and the crowd outside was bewildered; how was it possible? How was it that the Pope was a mother?

"But," said Rizhiner Rebbe, "it is known that everything is possible when it comes to the nations of the world, and the same goes for their Holy Scriptures."

Suddenly, the man who came to the Rebbe with a plea to ease his wife's labor pains realized that he had forgotten what he came

Prologue

for. He turned to the Rebbe and whispered: "Rebbe! How does this story relate to me, I wonder?"

"It has! It has!" said the Rebbe. "While you listened to the story quite intently, your wife delivered a healthy baby boy. So, go home and bring up your child steeped in our Jewish tradition."

Reb Motele Tchernobiler was amazed. "I am baffled," he said, "that you, Reb Yisroeltche found it appropriate to tell this particular story."

"Why are you so amazed Reb Motele?" Reb Rizhiner calmed him down. "The power of a story is mightier than the pen and one can always walk away enriched from a good story."

References

D. L. Meeker, *Tchernobyl—from the Rebbe's Courtyard*, vol. 1 (New York: Jewish Book Publishing Company, 1931) (published in Yiddish).

Mariangela Rinaldi and Mariangela Vicini, (2001). *Buon Appetito, Your Holiness*, translated from the Italian by Adam Victor. London: Pan Books.

chapter one

Her stepmother's rough hands pulled the comb through Agnes Johanna's knotted hair, while not bothering to hold on at the top as she tugged the wooden tines through. Crying silently, Agnes Johanna knew not to make sounds. That would just encourage more pain and berating. Her half-brother watched and laughed. Agnes Johanna showed him her fist tightly clenched in her lap at the ready to punch him when she got free.

Eleven-year-old Agnes Johanna had chores to do. The woman pushed her away saying, "Go do your work. First go to the abbey and pick up the grain they have for us. Don't tarry. Come right back to clean out the chicken coop and prepare the meal." To her half-brother she said nothing as he sat on the floor idly moving wooden figures around in mock battle. He smirked.

If I was a boy, she wouldn't treat me like this, Agnes Johanna thought as she picked up the basket kicking her half-brother as she passed by. He howled, but she was out the door before her stepmother could catch her.

She walked quickly to the monastery, hoping that one particular monk, a novice, was giving out provisions. He was always nice to her and gave her a wooden stool to sit on under the window of the classroom when she found time to listen. He gave her more grain than others so that he would be in her good graces, this girl who absorbed the lessons faster than any of the novices. He wanted to get to know her.

He was there. She blushed as she looked down at her feet. She held out her basket and he filled it with the grain she would later grind for bread. He touched her hand as she turned to go and looked directly into her eyes. "I thank you," she muttered blushing and turned around to see that his eyes followed her down the path. He nodded and half smiled.

Since she never received any positive attention at home, Agnes Johanna basked in the good nature of this novice. He was only a few years older than she, and his handsome profile and manner, and his attention to her, made her feel better than she had since her mother died.

She came here often whenever she could get away from the drudgery of her home. The monk let her listen in on the classes. He nurtured her desire to learn. Here she learned to read the Latin texts given to her by the kindly monk who was intrigued by her relentless questions. She read the bible, the commentaries, and anything he gave her. When she returned them, the monk questioned her, hardly believing that a young girl could comprehend the texts as fully as she did. Agnes Johanna's mind was quick and inquisitive, and this provided her with the desire to study and learn. It was something she knew she was good at, something that was hers all alone. She did not need the others in her house to praise her. She did not need their approval or their disappointment to know in her heart that she owned her mind and that no matter what, they could not take that away from her. Agnes Johanna escaped by reading the texts fluently and she was quick to understand the most complex of passages. Her stepmother and half-brother could not. Her prison was her home; her liberation was her mind.

Chapter One

Agnes Johanna kept her lessons from both parents, even her father who was remote and sad most of the time. He never got over the loss of her mother, so wrapped up in his own misery and the shrewish wife he now had that he paid little attention to her. Agnes Johanna was so used to this that rather than crave attention, she tried not to be seen and noticed by either of the adults in her home. If there were no chores, her stepmother would not even question where she was or what she was doing. No one cared as long as she did her work.

This would bother most children, but not her. She steeled herself to not be angry about it. She was neither envious, nor jealous, nor angry, nor lonely. Her feelings were numb and she was determined not to cry or show them that their behavior affected her in any way. She was good at hiding things. So good, in fact, that she internalized that it did not in the least bother her. Her demeanor was flat, aloof, and accepting.

The elderly monk lent her manuscripts that she hid behind a loose plank in a wall near her home. At night she would sneak outside with a candle to read the pages, eager to finish and exchange it for another from the abbey. She drank up everything he offered and he accommodated her by inclusion in classes with the young novices. This was a concession to her father who had been a traveling monk. He settled in this village where Agnes Johanna was born. When her mother died, Agnes Johanna was eight, and he found a woman to care for him and his young daughter. He found other work and never preached again. His dream of raising a family with his wife in some remote place where he would have a little congregation was unfulfilled. So he gave up.

The family had traveled from England to Germany and settled in Mainz because of the library and Benedictine Abbey. A younger Agnes Johanna would sit and listen to the lessons and sermons of her father memorizing passages from the scriptures and parroting them as some children recite songs and rhymes. When her mother became ill and died, her father no longer wanted to preach. But Agnes Johanna had already acquired a thirst for knowledge and the abbey was renowned for its teaching and piety.

At eleven, Agnes Johanna knew that her freedom to absorb lessons at the abbey was coming to a close. Twelve was the limit to the education allowed for girls. This was the only thing in her life that frightened her. No one said anything about her age and the end of the lessons, but she knew it was coming. So did the young novice. While it was not unusual to school girls, women had other roles in medieval society, and the boy knew that her opportunities were closing. Young girls her age were most often married off to bear children. He liked her and could tell from her demeanor that she liked him. *What,* he thought, *could I do to make us closer before someone suggested she become a nun?*

Agnes Johanna thought the nunnery was certainly not for her. Being cloistered in obedience went against all her underlying feelings of specialness in her intellect and her independence of thought. Obedience, while she outwardly complied, was just not ingrained in her psyche.

Her attraction to the novice cemented in her mind that she could never be celibate. Her liberation was through her education and learning, but the vehicle to do this had not crystallized as yet. Not until the novice started paying attention to her.

They met regularly on the lanes leading to the abbey. He knew when she would be sent to get grain, when she would come for new readings. Their chance meetings were nothing of the sort. She let him think they were. He did not let on that he planned his walks to coincide with her errands. They would nod at each other and pass without comment.

Chapter One

One day on a walk he did more than smile at her. He brought some bread and wine and asked, "Would you like to sit and share this with me?"

She looked around to make sure that it was she to whom he directed the question. With no one else near, she nodded. Flustered, she said, looking down, "Yes, I would."

Neither of these two young people had any experience with the opposite sex. He had been cloistered in the monastery for years, orphaned when he was four. His awareness of her at age twelve was visceral, something that he did not understand. Yet, he wanted to touch her hair and look into her eyes. Instead, he sat beneath a tree, broke his bread, and offered her the larger half.

"Here, I know you must be hungry." From a fold in his robe, he produced a bladder of wine made in the monastery. He took a long drink and offered it to her.

"Thank you." Agnes Johanna could not find her voice. She, who was quick to learn and to ask questions about what she read, did not know how to talk to this boy. So she fell back on what was easy for her.

"I saw you outside class yesterday. You did not come in. Why?" he asked.

"I had too many chores to do. I just exchanged my readings for others and had to go home," she offered.

"The class was interesting, but I had trouble with the interpretation of the passage. Could you help me to understand?"

"Of course," Agnes Johanna said looking into his kind face. This conversation she was comfortable with, and as she looked at the passage he referred to, she animatedly described the implications and the questions that the passage posed and patiently explained them to the novice.

He smiled and said, "You are so much better at this than I."

She looked away at a tree. No one had complimented her in this way before. The monk encouraged her, but praise was foreign.

He added, "Agnes Johanna, you are special. The work comes so easily to you. You should be the one apprenticed here, not me."

She decided to confide in this boy. "It will soon end you know. I have reached the age when the lessons will conclude and they will either marry me off or send me to a nunnery."

"No." He blurted this out as he reached for her hand. "I will not let that happen."

"What?" she said not fully understanding what he meant by that. He reached for her hand and she let him hold it close to his heart.

"I will talk to the monks and see what we can do. If they won't interfere, I will think of something. I will. I promise."

"My stepmother will be cross if I am gone much longer," Agnes Johanna added, looking away again at the mossy grass. "I have to get back."

She stood and brushed the leaves from her old clothes. He rose also, collected the bladder of wine, and handed her the unfinished bread.

As she turned to leave, he said, "Agnes Johanna, when I make a promise, I mean it. I will find a way. I want to make you happy, to see you smile, to nurture your gift. I will find a way to do that. Do you understand?"

Touched, she nodded and turned to quickly walk away.

chapter two

"Husband, we have to make arrangements for Agnes Johanna."

"What do you mean?" he asked, absently eating his dinner of bread, ale, and potatoes. "Has she not listened to you again?" He did not want to reprimand his daughter at all. She was overworked and he knew it.

"No. She is sometimes too fast with her work and goes skulking off somewhere, but no, that is not what I mean."

"Then what, woman? I am not a mind reader." He regretted this annoyance in his voice and knew she would exact punishment on him, verbally or otherwise, for speaking back to her.

"She has to be married off. Soon. Or you will have to visit the abbot to make arrangements for the nunnery. One or the other. You pick which."

"Married? She is a child."

"No, she is of age. We cannot house her much longer, and she is always causing tension here with the boy."

If you did not favor him so, maybe they would not be at war, he thought, but dared not say so out loud. "What should I do? What do you want me to do? Or, have you already made plans?" he asked.

"I have. There is a boy who is of age. The smith's son. He is apprenticed to his father and will have a position eventually in the ironworks. The mother came to me and asked about Agnes Johanna."

"I know who you speak of. He is one oaf of a boy, pockmarked and surly. Is that who you mean to couple with my Agnes Johanna?" he blurted out.

"It is him or the monastery. Pick one. Quickly so we are done with her." She turned and went out of their house, leaving him at the table to ponder his only daughter's fate.

He knew he had to visit the boy's father to see what they really intended, but he was equally sure that a young, uneducated smith was not what his daughter had in mind. Not at all. He lit his crude pipe and went out of the house to walk to the smith's home.

He knocked and asked if the smith was there. The big muscled man with hands like sandpaper came out and looked down at Agnes Johanna's father. Nodding, he beckoned him in for a drink of ale while motioning to his son to go outside and leave them alone.

The boy was almost as big as his father, equally grimy with dull eyes. He was illiterate and listened to his father faithfully. His muscles were honed on a forge, and he lumbered off in obedience.

"What do you have to say to me?" asked the smith as he laid the ale on the table.

"Our wives have talked recently about my daughter and your son," he mumbled, looking at the floor.

"Yes. My wife told me. So is it to be? Is that what you wish?" asked the smith.

Agnes Johanna's father looked up at the no-nonsense man sitting in front of him, his big dirty hands on the wooden table, oil and grease on his bare arms. Agnes Johanna's father said nothing.

The smith moved about in his wooden chair. It creaked under his weight, foretelling the physique of the son as he grew older. This uneducated man who toiled by his sweat was not what he and Agnes Johanna's mother had wanted when she was born. Not that

Chapter Two

he minded hard work and perseverance; it was just not anything he imagined for his daughter. He knew she was special. She was smart, and this family, this man, and his son were no match for her abilities and her thirst for knowledge. His daughter would not think kindly about this and would not tolerate such a match.

"Honestly, I do not know. I have yet to talk to Agnes Johanna. My wife sent me and she is not one to cross, but I will think about it. I just wanted you to know that I am leaving the decision up to Agnes Johanna. I know that is unusual, but she does have a mind of her own," he said.

"Yes. I have heard. I believe she has to be tamed. My son is strong enough to beat that out of her. I am agreeable. Let me know. It is time for him to make a match," said the smith.

Agnes Johanna's father stood, nodded to the man, and walked out to aimlessly wander the feudal streets and stave off the wrath of his wife who he was sure would be angry with him. She was always angry, but this would evoke unimaginable verbal wrath from her, screaming that would be heard by the entire village.

What will my daughter do when she hears about this? he thought. *I cannot give her to them. I cannot do this to her. I have to tell her so she can decide what to do.* By the time he arrived home, it was late and only Agnes Johanna was up. She was preparing to go outside to read the latest book from the monastery by candlelight. He came to the door as she was going out.

"Agnes Johanna, I have to talk to you alone."

"Yes, Father," she said as she looked up at his sad face.

He motioned for them to walk away from the house. When they were out of earshot of his wife, he said, "Daughter. There are plans afoot to marry you off to the smith's son."

"No," she blurted out with fear. "That ignorant dirty boy who can barely speak and clods about?"

"Wait. I am not going to let that happen. I just came from there and told the father that it was up to you. I knew what you would say. But Agnes Johanna, the alternative, now that you are eleven, is equally untenable. It is the nunnery if you do not marry. You know that and while not to your liking, it is a way for you to continue your education and you would have access to the writings you hold so dear."

"Father, I love you, but a nunnery is also not for me. I leave you either way I turn, so I am going to see what else is possible. Please do not tell your wife about our conversation as yet. Give me a few days before saying I reject both choices."

"Daughter, what is it you plan? Is this something I should worry about? Do you want to tell me?"

"No, Father. She will find out if I tell you. Just know that I will be safe. I will be protected. I will make you proud of me."

He had tears in his eyes as she said this, and he responded, "I will do everything to put her off." He looked away saying, "You are going to leave me. I understand. Go with God my child." He turned and hugged her and kissed her cheek. He hoped that his only daughter would find happiness and that she would be safe, whatever she planned to do.

This is too terrible to even think about. I will never give in. I do not want to leave Father. I would miss him terribly. But I cannot go along with my stepmother's plan. I would rather die than suffer that fate, she thought.

She and her father arrived home, and she waited until he had settled in for the night, then she went in quietly, took a burlap bag and threw her few belongings into it. She gathered the papers borrowed from the monastery and some parchment and quills, and then set off in the dark. It was almost time for the morning liturgy, the lauds.

Chapter Two

Agnes Johanna walked to the monastery and hoped that she could speak to the novice, or at least have someone deliver a note to him. There was very little activity, but one monk was readying to call the other monks to prayer. She walked in, a common sight since she often appeared there unannounced, and handed him the note and returned the papers she borrowed. Recognizing her, he nodded. She asked him to deliver her missive to the particular novice. She then turned and headed out to the woods where they often met.

She waited quite a while as the day warmed and thought he might not be able to come to her. Just when she was ready to set out on her own, he appeared on the road carrying a burlap bag with some food for them.

"I brought this for you. It will make traveling better." He handed her a monk's robe, black like the Benedictine order, with a hair shirt and cowl. "You cannot travel as a woman. It is too dangerous. Wear this and people will think you are just another monk traveling from one monastery to another."

Holding up the garb, she quickly understood the implication. She could travel as a man in a man's world, but she could not do so as a woman. They could go into public places and no one would question them or assume she was a woman in disguise. She smiled at the subterfuge. She liked this idea.

As she changed into the robe, he told her that he had a plan. They would travel to Fulda and apprentice themselves to the big monastery there. Since they were both literate and could scribe, there was a center of scholarship and a monastery where they could live and study. The trip was one hundred miles. It would take some time to get there, and they could not risk being discovered or have Agnes Johanna forced to return.

"I have a letter of introduction from the abbot here. They

should welcome us both and since we can contribute, they should make us a part of their community," he said smiling.

"You are clever," she said as she tied the waist of her robe and donned the sandals. Her hair was a problem, so she secured it in the folds of the scapula and raised the cowl around her head. "This is how we will travel, and we can beg for food along the way. No one turns down pious monks traveling to another monastery."

"Yes, that is what I think too. You will get to study further once we get there. Their library is renowned," he said knowing that this was her goal.

She turned in the direction of her home and glanced back. The look in her eyes was one of determination without any sign of regret.

"You cannot call me Agnes Johanna any longer."

"What would you like then, young man?" he asked.

"Gilbert, how about that? Gilbert and Henricus, two novices traveling together."

He nodded. "Yes. Shall we be off?" He turned to look at her more closely, staring in that strong face, her chin forward; they set off down the road. She did not ask how long it would take. She knew it was far and she was prepared for the trip. He added, "I brought manuscripts for you to read on the way."

"You have thought of everything. We need to get away from here as quickly as possible. I do not want anyone following us or questioning where I am."

He will protect me on the trip. He is a man. Really a boy. I have to let him lead me. I do like the way he protects me. He seems kind and sincere and I think he likes me enough, she thought.

No more stepmother, no more toiling away for her. No marrying the smith's son or going to the nunnery. She was taking the first steps of a life adventure and she was intent on making the most of it.

Chapter Three

One hundred miles on foot with no money and no food was what the two travelers faced.

"We may not get far today, but I think we had better travel off the main road," said Henricus.

"Yes," she nodded, "we likely could meet someone so close to home that may recognize us since many of the pious often come here to study or meet with the abbot. We should be careful so as not to be sighted."

"Let us walk through the woods on a parallel line. It will be slower yet easier to hide if someone approaches."

They veered into the woods and went a few miles, stopping to eat the meager provisions he brought from the monastery. The weather was mild this time of year, but winter was coming and a wave of cold air from the north would likely come before they got to their destination.

"Eat. This may be the last food until we can safely get back to the road."

"That is fine. I am used to meager provisions."

They ate the rest of the food in silence, each pondering the enormity of their decision to leave Mainz and travel together to Fulda and a new life. She was all hope that this would provide an opportunity to expand her knowledge and pursue her studies. He already loved her and was certain she cared for him. Feeling sure he could protect her and get her to their destination, his demeanor was of protection of this precious fellow traveler.

"We had better be going. I am not sure how far we can walk through these woods, but in order to make this trip easier by tomorrow we should veer back onto the road." Henricus stood and put out his hand to help her up off the leafy ground where they ate. She took his hand and thought, *He is so kind and protective. Never would he betray my identity, but instead he would do anything necessary to let me rise above my female condition. I will do what is necessary to make him happy.* "You are the kindest person I know," she uttered.

"Come, we should find protection before night falls."

They walked another few hours when, as it does in fall, the cool of night started to close in. Finding a shady area beneath trees, he piled leaves on the ground for them to lie on and lit a fire as the cool air of night engulfed them. When the fire died down, she moved closer to him for warmth. He put his arm around her cradling her body and breathing in her scent.

Up early, they set off and by midday made their way back toward the road. Henricus thought they were safe now, but of course no one was safe from the bandits on the road and the perils of traveling alone. They only had their monkish garb to ward off danger and sometimes, they had heard through stories of travelers, this was not protection enough.

To pass the time Gilbert, the name she now thought of as her own, discussed some passages with Henricus of scripture or topics of concern she had. She wanted to probe him for any information he had discussed in his learning that she was not privy to. Although she read the texts, she could not always answer questions she had of interpretation and dogma. Her questions were endless, and it was often difficult for him to follow her line of reasoning.

He laughed at her constant queries. "We will be at Fulda soon

Chapter Three

enough and you will have all your questions answered. I cannot enlighten you fully. I can only give you what I have learned as a novice, but as you see, you are already surpassing me in understanding. You probably will tire of me as you advance in your studies." He looked forlorn.

She was sensitive not to hurt this boy's feelings. She liked him. He was her knight, so she said, "Henricus. Never say that. No matter what, I will not tire of my protector. I will not tire of you." She looked down and blushed realizing that indeed a love for him was growing and all maidenly fear and shame was put aside. Looking up into his eyes, she smiled as he bent down to kiss her. She let him hold her close to him.

Hearing some horses snorting, they quickly broke off as a group of travelers headed toward them on the road. The two moved back toward the trees, but they had been seen. They lowered their heads and Gilbert pulled the cowling closer around her head. The riders passed close and one said, "Much farther to Mainz?"

Henricus shook his head indicating no. The riders were ill kempt and eyed them suspiciously, circling them with the horses. The two moved closer together and backed up to a tree.

"How far then?" the man demanded gruffly.

"One day by foot, sir."

"You two from there?"

"No. Just passed through," Henricus said, not wanting them to talk about the two novices they met on the road when they got to Mainz. "We are poor novices who came from the north and are walking to a monastery on a pilgrimage. Is there any lodging farther on this road? Someone who might give us some bread and a place to sleep?"

"Yes. A small farmhouse a ways ride that way." He pointed back toward where the riders had come from. "When the road forks, go right and it is not far." He sneered as he said this, which aroused suspicion from Henricus.

The man turned to the others and shook his head from left to right. Off they went, each one in turn staring at the two waifs on the road as they passed close to them on their horses.

"I think they wanted to rob us. There are many bandits on the road. I will do the talking if anyone else speaks to us. If you have to answer, keep it brief and try to talk in a lower voice. Do not look in anyone's eyes. You are still too beautiful even under that cloak. I do not want anyone to suspect you are anything except a young novice. Keep your hands in the robe also. They are delicate."

"Yes, and callused. Monks hands are smoother. That will go away with time," she said looking at the red spots from cleaning clothes and making soap with lye.

"You are beautiful to me. And only I will be able to know that and see you for whom you really are. Let's go. Maybe the farmer will let us stay the night and give us some bread."

As they walked, Gilbert, nee Agnes Johanna, struggled with her new identity. *Are you born thinking of yourself one way and that is the way you see yourself and present yourself to others always? Or, can you change your self-image and forever after take on the identity of the other?* she pondered. She wanted to talk to Henricus about this, but she was not sure he would understand that the change from female to male outwardly would change the way she interacted with others and the world. Who was she and what would she become? Her eleven years of being female amounted to very little opportunity to do the thing that mattered to her the most: to study and learn. But this new idea, this change, meant that there would be no obstacle in the path of her reaching for knowledge.

They walked on and when they got to the fork, they veered right as nightfall was coming. Not far, they saw a farmhouse and walked

Chapter Three

openly up to the broken gate. A farmer came around the hut with a pitchfork scowling and angry at the intrusion, way beyond what was necessary. He yelled, "Off my land. Get away."

"Sir, we mean no harm. We are two novices on a pilgrimage to Fulda. Could we bed down in shelter just for this one night? Possibly ask you for some bread to eat? We do not want any trouble. We are just travelers who are very tired," said Henricus.

The farmer looked at them, warily pointing his pitchfork. Both Henricus and Gilbert backed up. "We are scribes making our way to a monastery far away. We are just seeking shelter from the elements. Please sir," added Gilbert.

The farmer looked at her curiously and realized that this monk was a beautiful child and no danger to him. He looked back at his hut where his wife was cleaning the mess the bandits made, happy that she was unharmed. Often the bandits raped the women on their travels, but for some reason she was spared.

"You can stay with the pigs just for one night. Then you have to leave before dawn. For bread, you can help me clean up. A group of bandits came not long ago and took my best provisions, but I can give you each a piece of bread my wife is making now."

"We saw them on the road, but they let us pass. We have nothing of value to them I imagine. Nothing at all," Henricus said.

"Thank you, sir," said Gilbert. "What would you like us to do first?"

"Repair that fence first and reattach the gate. Tools are in the storage hut. Then go out back and catch the chickens and pen them. Those men let them loose just for spite when they left. I will bring you the bread when it is cool." He turned and walked off toward the house.

"Sometimes my softness helps," she smiled.

"Come on. I never caught a chicken before," he said.

"Ah. That will be your lesson for this day! A skill you will acquire that you will not easily forget," she teased.

After their chores were done, they cleared out an area next to the pig sty and piled leaves under some burlap bags. They sat down exhausted from walking all day and then fixing the fence, catching chickens, and cleaning the sty area. Oblivious to the odor of the pigs, they fell asleep immediately and woke to the sound of the farmer's voice telling them that the bread was ready.

"Here is a loaf for your work and a flask of wine." He started to turn away without saying anything else, yet looked back and said, "Be careful on your travels. It is a long way to Fulda. There are many to take advantage of you. You are both young. Beware." Then he turned and walked off.

They slept fitfully, each one thinking about the perils ahead. Waking at first light, they stood and prepared to set off. There was some bread left that Henricus put under his robe. They finished the wine and went back toward the road for another day of walking, not knowing what would happen on the way.

The sky was gray. A cold wave was on its way. They would have to seek shelter that night, but how far they would have to walk was unknown. They were young and strong but hungry most of the time, and as day wore on, clouds came and the sky darkened. They saw no one on the way, and Henricus was getting concerned about that evening. Where would they find shelter, food, and a place to be safe before nightfall? He did not want to worry her, so he turned and said, "We will walk farther today. There must be a town up ahead where we can stop and spend the night. Let's speed up a little to cover more distance this day."

She nodded, deep in thought about a passage she was reading. Putting the papers under her robe, she stepped up to him and matched his pace as they walked down the road.

chapter four

Walking down the Roman roads was a dangerous thing for men to do. It was more treacherous for two young novice monks with no protection. By evening, they had walked about six miles on the rutted path and a chill was setting in. They were lucky that there were no others traveling on this path today, but there was also no shelter anywhere on the route.

"Can you go still a little farther?" asked Henricus who was anxious to find shelter so they would not have to sleep in the woods.

Although tired and hungry, she nodded yes.

On they went in the darkness hoping that they would find someplace to sleep for the night. They wrapped their cloaks closer around their faces as the half-moon rose to give them enough light to show the way.

"I smell something. Smoke, I think," Gilbert said.

"Yes, I think so. It is in that direction. Follow me."

They discerned a moonlit lane off to the left. They followed for a time and came across a small hamlet with huts and a surrounding field that was planted with grains, barley for bread, and ale and peas and beans to put into stews with onions, garlic, leeks, cabbage, and legumes. The sheep looked up as they approached. No one was out, all in their huts after a day of labor.

"I do not want to scare them. That would be dangerous. It is dark already and they probably are asleep. Perhaps we could just lie down near the sheep for warmth and see if they could give us bread in the morning," Henricus said.

Gilbert was so tired that she just nodded and found a spot protected by the side of a feedbox and lay down, asleep immediately. He sat down next to her, pulled his robe closer, and slept close.

At dawn, they awoke to prodding by the sharecropper who was holding a stick with a metal hoe attached.

They opened their eyes with a start, stood up, and began explaining as the farmer held out his stick at arm's length.

"We are sorry sir. Just seeking shelter on our pilgrimage to Fulda."

"Yes, please, we mean no harm. It was just late and we did not want to awaken you."

"We are sorry sir. We were just cold and . . ."

"Where are you coming from?" asked the farmer.

"Far north. We are going to study and be illuminators," Henricus offered.

"Go on then. Get going."

The two started to turn and walk off when Gilbert looked back and said, "Sir, could you spare some meager bread to sustain us this day? Or some porridge? We have not eaten in a long time and have many more days of travel."

The farmer eyed them and said, "Perhaps. You are doing God's work. I will see what I can offer. No porridge, but I may have part of a loaf left from yesterday. Wait here."

He opened the gate for the sheep to graze on the nearby grasses and went into the hut, emerging quickly with the partially eaten loaf. "Here." He held the bread out to Gilbert.

"Thank you, sir. May we fill our bladders with water from the well?" interrupted Henricus to distract this man from staring at Gilbert's hands.

Chapter Four

"Yes. I have some barley ale also. Would you rather that to drink with the bread?"

"Yes, please," said Gilbert as the farmer went back inside and emerged with a flagon for them to share.

They sipped some ale and ate a piece of bread, filling their bladders with the remaining ale that they diluted with well water to take with them.

"Would you know how far it is to the next town?" asked Henricus.

"A day's walk, I think, by the road. I have only been there once."

By now some of the workers from the other huts were coming out to eye the travelers. Gilbert pulled the cloak closer around her head and silently indicated to Henricus that she was done speaking. The workers came over to see if the farmer needed their help. He held up his hand to stop them and looked down the road as Henricus and Gilbert turned to leave. As they walked off, the group was told, "Back to work," by the farmer.

So distrustful, thought Gilbert. *Such a hard life and they trust no outsiders. Not even novice monks who look unthreatening and seek to spread the word of the Lord. What could enlighten them that not all men want something from them? That only belief can keep them safe for eternity? Maybe those questions will be answered when I know more and study more.*

"To the town. It is early so we should make it by nightfall if we keep up a good pace," said Henricus. His only thoughts were how to keep them safe on this quest. Matters of dogma and religious discourse were not a priority. He felt in need of protecting his charge and starting out in a new place where she would flourish and look upon him with kindness and closeness. To be with her always was what he wanted. At fourteen going on fifteen he was middle-aged, and he knew he wanted to spend all his time with her.

By the afternoon, they had made good progress. But the weather was changing and within an hour, clouds replaced the scant light coming through the trees and the temperature dropped. A light rain during the morning turned to sleet, then snow, and the two kept their hands deep inside their black robes to keep them warm, their hoods protecting their heads from the wet snow. By the time they got close to the town, water had soaked their cloaks and almost penetrated the thick woven garments. They hurried along in silence, each conserving their warmth.

Up ahead, off the road, was a rudimentary series of huts serving as the village. In them was a blacksmith, a miller, and a larger edifice serving as a tavern and general provision store. There was no window or door, just an animal skin hung over an opening.

The two entered gingerly and moved closer to the fire in the corner to dry out. They held their cold hands out to the flames and tried to quell their chattering teeth. Turning around, they did the same for the back of their robes, looking up to see that they had an audience watching them. There were ten or more men drinking ale at wooden tables. A barmaid was carrying flagons to tables of shouting men who reached for her arms or teased her as she made her way around the crowded room. Some were eating food, but most were just drinking.

Gilbert had never been in a tavern before. Always curious, her eyes grew wide as she took in the scene, watching the men grope for the barmaid as she passed or swatting her rear, playfully flirting with her. It was hard for her to look away. Noting this, Henricus whispered, "Do not look directly at them. Let me talk. I will see if we can stay for the night and perhaps get something to eat."

The barmaid walked over to the tavern keeper, who was busy telling the men to keep their hands off his woman. Noticing the

Chapter Four

two monks only after the barmaid told him they were by the fire and pointed directly at them, the man came out from behind the bar and approached them. "Not good for business to have religious types here. Stops the flow; know what I mean? Get on with you," he said gruffly.

"Sir, we have no place to warm ourselves and are just novices walking to Fulda. Please, can we just dry out and perhaps stay in that corner for the night, out of the elements? Please, sir," said Henricus.

The man looked at him and realized that the other was just a child, old enough to be a novice, pretty for a boy, but quiet and not likely to bother anyone. Some of Gilbert's hair had come out from under her cowl hanging in long wet strands around her face. The tavern keeper kept staring at her. Henricus was getting worried. He knew some men liked young boys. He had heard this from the monks who often touched the novices in secret.

Henricus stepped out in front of Gilbert and said, "Just a while longer, sir. Just to dry off some and then we will be gone."

The tavern keeper turned from Gilbert to him and said, "You can stay the night by the fire. Stay out of the way until everyone leaves for the night. I will have some ale sent over to warm you."

"And some bread?" said Gilbert emphatically in a low voice. She was behind Henricus looking down at her feet.

The man nodded and turned, walking away.

They sat near the fire, sipping the ale and eating the stale bread given to them by the barmaid who eyed them with suspicion. She passed by often trying to get a better look at Gilbert, and Henricus overheard her say something to one of the men about why such a pretty boy would go into the monastery.

"Take out your prayer sheets and start to read in a low voice to yourself. Look like you are praying. Show them you are learned, and maybe they will be fearful of us. The only thing these people fear is the afterlife, hell, and damnation. Let's see if they lose interest. We can leave before dawn, if necessary. I think the snow has stopped."

She nodded, took out her prayers, and started to read in Latin while thinking, *There are many more days of this. Not knowing where we will end up or who we might encounter. We have to have a better plan than just begging for occasional pieces of bread and ale to drink.* Tomorrow she would discuss this with Henricus. Perhaps they could tarry somewhere and earn enough to buy provisions to sustain them. It would add days to their trip, but they would not die of starvation and the elements.

When the last patron had left, the barmaid cleaned up the tables and carried the used steins back to the bar. Gilbert stood and asked, "Can we clean these for you in exchange for some food and some provisions to take on our trip? We would be working for our food. Please. Good deeds are rewarded and you would be helping two novices on their pilgrimage."

The barmaid turned and looked Gilbert in the eye. Where men see men, she thought that the size and demeanor of this novice was different. She stared with her hands on her hips and said, "Child, be careful. Your disguise is not complete. You walk like a woman, your voice is too high, and you are not aggressive enough to handle men like this. I will help you, but be gone in the morning and take care in the future."

"Yes ma'am," said Gilbert in a voice as low as she could.

"And trim your hair so it does not stick out."

Gilbert nodded.

After cleaning all the steins and lining them up on the bar,

Chapter Four

picking up the chairs and stacking them on the tables, and sweeping the dirt floor of the tavern, she and Henricus sat down in front of the fire and fell asleep.

In the morning they found a burlap bag with bread, ale, and some porridge in bowls, which they ate before leaving for the walk to Fulda.

chapter five

It was cold and damp as they set out, and after walking for most of the morning, they stopped to rest near a lake. Gilbert needed to wash herself as it was the end of her time of the month. The rags she used were soaked and she had to clean and replace them. It was cold water, but she was determined to cleanse herself.

"Henricus, I am going to the lake to wash. It is a necessity." She did not wait for a response, but stood up and walked away. At the water's edge, she took off her black robe and the undercloth, removed the rags, and knelt down straddling a rock. Immersing herself partway in the water, she washed, rinsed out the rags, and put them on a branch to dry. Although she was cold, the sun was peering through the arms of a nearby tree, so she waded in up to her hips. The cold water took her breath away and as she turned back to the shore, she saw Henricus standing there watching her.

Blushing, she said, "I asked you to wait."

"I just wanted to make sure you were all right," he said staring at her body.

He held her undercloth up to her as she emerged from the water shivering as much from having this boy look at her as from the cold. He slipped it over her head, cradling her body close to his as she turned around. He bent down to kiss her, and she let him. His hands moved across her back and down, and she was warmed by his closeness. *I like this boy and I want to please him*, she thought.

Chapter Five

Spreading her black robe on the ground, Henricus lay down with her at the edge of the forest ignoring the cold air of impending winter. They were lost in their first exploration of each other's bodies. He fumbled with her cloth, but natural urges overcame their awkward introduction to sex. It was over quickly, neither of them experienced, but it presaged the future, and they vowed to be together no matter what their future held.

"We cannot stay here," he said. "We have to keep going and find shelter for tonight." As he said this, he looked in her eyes and kissed her again, running his hands through her long hair. She suddenly was reminded of the barmaid's warning and the telltale signs of female trappings.

"I know. I will be ready quickly." She stood, retrieved the rags, and put her undercloth back on, and he held the robe out for her. "Not yet," she said. "I have to cut my hair. Give me your knife."

Henricus took out the small blade he had tied to the rope over his undercloth and handed it to her. She carried it down to the water's edge and cut her long hair to make it look more like that of a boy. She threw the tresses into the water and watched them float away. Turning back, she walked to him and handed him his knife, which he reattached to his makeshift inside belt. He held her robe out so she could put it over her head. She raised the cowling, picked up her staff as he did his, and off they went, holding hands this time.

By late afternoon, they started passing more huts and knew they were getting closer to the land holdings around Fulda. It was still a few days off, yet they were aware that more abundant property meant an increased likelihood of bandits on the road.

"I think we should take a detour again, just to be sure we are safe. If we walk a few more leagues, we can go back to the road and see if one of the planters will give us shelter for the night."

She nodded absently. All she could think about were the events of that day and of the possibility that this boy would take care of her and that they would continue their charade so she could study and learn, her real goal. *I do care for him, but my purpose is to learn more, to learn everything. To get past the circumstances of my life and never look back as I become what was to be taken away from me in Mainz.*

They wandered west and followed a parallel route until the skies started to darken and the cold became more intense. As they walked east, they heard voices. Not far ahead was a small group of men, dirty, boisterous, standing beside their mounts, talking in quiet voices. The two travelers crouched down behind a large tree and Henricus motioned for her to be quiet and not move.

All of a sudden they were yanked from their hiding place by two burly men who pulled them up by their arms and dragged them to the others.

"What is this?" asked the obvious leader of the group.

"Off in the woods, listening to us. Want me to get rid of them?"

"They are monks. Harmless or not, no good having them go ahead and alert the farmer. Keep them with us, walking behind. Almost dark. We need to find a spot for the night and before dawn we go. Tie their hands and take their staffs."

The men who found them showed a slight tinge of fear as they tied the hands of religious monks in front. Although lawless, their fear of the Almighty was not eliminated by their current behavior. They followed orders, fearful of their leader more than of the Lord, but they did it reluctantly.

Near a fairly protected area, the bandits tied their horses to a tree and one of them lit a fire. Henricus and Gilbert were pushed to the ground not far from the flame. The men made a rudimentary camp and cooked a rabbit, which one of them had killed during the day, in a pot with greens and roots, while the two monks stole glances at each other, looking for a way to escape.

Chapter Five

One of the guards placed a small portion of the stew in front of each of the prisoners. He untied their hands and walked back to the flame to finish his share. Henricus and Gilbert ate hungrily as they whispered to each other to devise a plan of escape.

Hearing their whispers, the leader walked over and kicked Henricus. "Quiet or I will separate your head from your body." He tied their bonds anew, walked away, and nodded to one of the others to watch them and keep them quiet.

"Can I stand up and go near the tree over there," asked Henricus sometime later.

The oaf looked at Henricus and nodded as he picked his teeth with his knife.

Henricus walked over to the tree, followed by the man who also had to watch over Gilbert. She made some movement as if to stretch out her legs and he thought she too was going to stand up, so he moved closer to her saying, "Don't move. Keep still and quiet." She nodded.

Henricus returned and sat down next to her, his fingers tightly held in a fist. He closed his eyes and Gilbert followed his lead, feigning sleep. Their guard got bored and went for another drink of ale and, as he turned, Henricus let the knife slip down to his hand and cut his ties. He rolled over before the guard returned and loosened hers.

It was well past midnight and from what they could hear, the bandits would leave before dawn. Everyone was asleep, including their guard. They rose quietly, inching back, untied all the horses, and went as far into the woods as they could run. The stirring of the horses woke the men who cared less about them than retrieving their mounts. Chaos reigned as the men scrambled after the horses and the two monks hid in a large clump of trees well away from the campsite.

"We should go warn the farmers before they attack," Gilbert said.

Henricus, having just gotten them out of danger, looked at her as she proposed they wade into the very place the bandits would attack.

She read his face in the moonlight and said, "It is a good deed. Isn't that what we are about? Come." She walked off toward the farmer's field closest to where they were.

He followed. He would follow wherever she wanted to go: Fulda and beyond.

They ran up to the farmer's hut and called out to him. He came out quickly and ready to hurt the strangers. Seeing the monks, he stopped and stepped back toward his door.

"We mean no harm, but we just escaped from bandits who are near. They intend to come here to loot before dawn. You have to prepare and tell your neighbors," said Henricus.

The farmer went to the bell hanging near and rang it loudly. He and his neighbors devised a warning system that could be heard in the still of the night when danger was near. "Here, keep ringing," the farmer said to Gilbert.

She pulled the cord clanging the bell for a long time and heard other bells being rung, one after the other, warning other farmers farther and farther from the danger. *Clever devising this system to protect them*, she thought.

The bandits by now had caught up with the horses and were preparing for the attack when they heard the bells going off. The element of surprise was taken away and they did not dare attack farmers prepared to fend them off. "Damn those monks. They must have told them. Who was watching them?" the leader yelled and nodded at one of his loyal followers.

Fear clouded over the face of the one with the last watch. He

Chapter Five

backed up across the lane, and as his hand went to the hilt of his sword, he was skewered from behind by one of the men who got the signal from the leader.

They took the reins of his horse and led him off as the man lay writhing on the ground. No one looked back or dared to try to save him. They rode off in the direction of another hamlet of farmers to the north.

The farmer prepared anyway, giving each a pitchfork to use in the event of an attack. The monks waited with the others, the farmer, his wife and sons, for the bandits to get there. After some time, they realized no one was coming.

"What did you do to them? They usually come anyway, but often we ring the bells after one of us has been hit." said the farmer.

"Well. I untied their horses so I presume they had to retrieve them first. By then your bell ringing would have reached them and the surprise was gone from their intentions," said Gilbert.

Not having slept all night was exhausting. The farmer sensed this and told them they could step down and, if they wanted, sleep for a time in the shed near the hut. They did, too tired from the stress and wonder of the day to do anything but close their eyes and drift off.

Sleeping well into the morning, Gilbert woke first. She moved closer to Henricus and hugged him. As he opened his eyes, he smiled because they were safe for another day, but he was anxious to get away from the farmer so they could be alone once again.

The farmer gave them food, ale, and a rag filled with more bread and dried meat to chew on until they found other nourishment. Thanking them for the warning, he bade them safe trip and said it was just a few more days, two at most, to Fulda.

chapter six

It was a cold crisp morning at the cusp of winter. The leaves that had fallen on the ground crunched under their feet as they walked on toward Fulda. Wanting to be alone, they started down the road, but the proximity to the monastery prevented that. The road was full of others making their way to the same destination. The multitude of fellow travelers included farmers taking their crops for sale in the market that arose around the monastery, sheep farmers taking wool to weavers, pilgrims making their way to pray, and monks who sought guidance and learning at Fulda's most venerable and eminent library. There was no time to be alone. They walked along in silence, keeping up the persona of pious monks and staved off their desires until they could hide the truth of their circumstance from the world once more.

Making good progress, they walked with the others until dark. They were now a half day from the monastery and a makeshift group of travelers were gathering for the night. Preparations were underway for a meal of wine, bread, and thin soup that was equally shared by all. Everyone contributed to the pot: some oats, barley, garlic, cabbage and onions, and plants found along the way.

Gilbert, having grown up with a conventional wisdom of herbs, knew she had to prevent pregnancy, and as the others went along looking for foodstuffs, she sought certain traditional herbs that she had observed or knew about from lore. From the time of ancient Greece, silphium, a giant fennel, was used and depicted on Grecian coins as a contraceptive, but in this Germanic land, she went

Chapter Six

searching for the seeds of Queen Anne's lace and pennyroyal, both thought to reduce fertility. This was known primarily from observing that animals who ate these plants did not produce offspring.

Returning to the group, she placed the seeds in her pouch and added wild onions to the pot warming over the fire.

"What did you find?" Henricus asked.

"Something for us and something for them."

"For us. Don't you think we should equally contribute since we will be eating their food?" he asked perplexed.

She smiled. "No. This is for us," she said showing him the seeds she found. "I do not want there to be any complications. No children. It just is not in my plan. I cannot be caught or I will not be allowed to stay with you," she added.

Seeing a flash of sadness about him, she said, "I want us to be free to study, to love each other as we wish. We cannot do that if I do not protect myself. I am a woman and am vulnerable. You do want to be with me, don't you, Henricus? I want you. But we need to be careful."

"Yes, I see," he said, holding her arm tenderly.

She looked at him and said, "Soon, but not now. There are too many eyes about. By tomorrow we will be in Fulda in our own cell. We will be alone to do as we wish. Carefully, so I am not exposed. Can you do that? Can you see me all day and only be ourselves at night? Can you Henricus?"

He nodded, unable to speak. He would wait for her and keep their secret.

By early light, the fires had been doused, and the pilgrims started the last leg of their journey to Fulda. They traveled along the Fulda River until the monastery loomed ahead, the river serving as a moat, and the volcanic mountains around protecting what was a fortress in earlier times. From the time of Pippin, the father of Charlemagne, nearly seventy years before, when control was taken away from Mainz and Boniface's relics were interred at Fulda, the communal identity of this Carolingian town adhered to the Rule of Benedict under the authority of Rome. The Carolingian Renaissance culminating in the Aachen Reform Councils of 816 established the Rule of Benedict followed in Fulda.

Henricus and Gilbert knew what this meant. The monastic rules of chastity and obedience, mutual control, and correction were the traditions that they were outwardly prepared to surrender to. No meat, drink or wine, a life of service to teach the youth, and the infusion of all into the established network of knowledge, priests, books, and devoting their lives to His cause were needed to remain in Fulda. At least openly. In practice, the monks used their standards and way of life as a mode of infusing in the local population an adherence to behaviors that transmitted messages using relics, liturgy, and religious art to control the behavior and thoughts of the people. In private, there were many transgressions as they lived their lives in service. This Gilbert knew from her experience in Mainz. It was what she counted on to live her life with access to the knowledge she sought.

As they approached, the farmers and millers went one way, the pilgrims to the church center, and Gilbert and Henricus sought out the monastery quarters where they hoped to get an audience with the abbot himself, Maurus Magentius Rabanus, the most learned man of his time.

They entered the monastery, more like a citadel than a hermitage due to its history, and sought out a monk. Staring up at the turrets, protection in times past of invasion from the battles waged in this area, a lone penitent came over and asked, "Can I aid you, brothers?"

"We have come from Mainz," said Henricus. "We are novices

Chapter Six

who seek further learning and service. I am Henricus and this is Gilbert. We are here to serve and have been recommended by the abbot at Mainz. We are both literate yet unfinished. Further study and service to your collective is what we wish."

Gilbert, reluctant to speak as yet, looked down at her sandals in obeisance.

"Follow me. I am Thomas. I will take you to the prior."

Walking behind Thomas in silence, the two stole glances at each other, their hands tucked in the folds of their cloaks.

Rabanus, the prior of Fulda, was famous. He had established and enforced a strict life for the clergy whose responsibilities extended to the life of the town that surrounded the monastery and spread its arms throughout the area.

Thomas nodded to the monks gathered outside the room where Rabanus was presiding, one after the other entering and leaving with instructions concerning land, farmers, monks, punishment, rewards, and general operations of this fiefdom.

They waited some time outside the room, standing quietly in a corner, not daring to speak to each other. Finally, Thomas came over to them after talking to the monk serving as gatekeeper to the prior and nodded for them to follow the prior's attendant into the prior's presence.

Rabanus was stern looking, his skull cap covering the circle of shaved hair as was the style. He wore a simple cloak typical of the Benedictines, and he was deep in thought writing something for the waiting monk to take from him. When he finished, he looked up and inspected the two novices.

He stood and came from behind his desk, walked around them, then said, "You have come here to learn, to study. We have simple rules here. Everyone works. We train monks, we sustain ourselves by working the land, we have no servants so some of the monks cook, others build cells for the monks to live in, we teach children in the village, and we adhere to prayer. We are the mirror that the locals look to so that they can have a pious life. What are your skills? Where shall we place you if you want to stay here?"

Gilbert looked up at him and said, "We can write and scribe. Both of us. I can also illuminate. I can read Latin and Greek also."

"And you?" asked Rabanus, looking at Henricus.

"I am fluent in Latin, my Greek is less advanced, but I also can scribe and have had experience in Mainz. I did miniatures and rubricatores there when I was not studying."

"But we can also do any kind of labor you need. We are young and strong," added Gilbert.

Rabanus turned his attention to her. He stared for a long time, and feeling her face flushing, Gilbert turned her eyes away, afraid to be found out for what she really was and end her quest for what was so close now. She desperately wanted to study here, under Rabanus.

"We can always use new scribes. My purpose is to not only duplicate the holy books, but I am finishing an encyclopedia and working on poems and need helpers. If you are quick of mind, I can use you. Otherwise, you will be assigned to other tasks and chores."

He turned to his attendant and said, "Show them to the novice's cells. I will let you know what their duties are in the morning." He turned and went back behind the table, picking up his quill and not looking up as they were escorted out.

The attendant called Thomas over and told him to find cells for them in the novice area.

"There are very few," said Thomas. "More are being built, but we have had many novices of late."

"Then they can share," said the attendant, turning back to the room where Rabanus was calling to him for another task.

Chapter Six

Henricus and Gilbert could not be happier with this arrangement. They followed Thomas to a row of cells. He opened a door and inside this very small space were two pallets, two wooden stools, and a washstand. Straw covered the floor, and a cross hung on the wall.

"This will be yours. Follow me and I will show you the rest of the monk's quarters."

They followed in silence because it was eerily quiet here. There was no noise, no talking in this wing. Occasionally whispered voices could be heard, but that was all. There was a larger room for the novices where silence was self-enforced. The refectory was decorated with large statues of the twelve apostles, and farther on they went down stone steps to the underground prisons where disobedient monks were buried alive. Up again, they entered the library where at least sixty scribes worked day and night on parchments and annotations of relics and feats of the saints.

Gilbert was in awe as she scanned the parchments lining the walls of this venerable place. Here she could study and expand her knowledge. She wanted to labor here.

Thomas said, "Let us go back to the cells. Prayer is followed by dinner. We rise early for prayer, and then you will find out where you are to go and what work you will do. You are free to study in your cell and will be instructed what to read by a senior monk."

He left them at the door, they went in, and in the frenzy of elation that they were now really here and the good fortune that they were in the same cell, Henricus took her arm and pulled her to him and gave her a long kiss. Over the next hours they explored each other's bodies, careful not to make noises that would attract someone to the door. As a precaution, he put the stool in front of the door so that no one could come in and surprise them.

chapter seven

Henricus and Gilbert woke to the Vespers bell at 4 p.m. They arose and quickly donned their cloaks and hurried out of their cell to the service in the large hall that accommodated all the monks and novices. Rabanus led the prayers and recitations, one of two that required all attend in person, the other being Prime at 6 a.m. All the other prayer times, the other six, were for private recitation. The Cantor, leader of the choir, conducted a small group of monks in song.

All work ceased when it was prayer time. The monks were required to stop what they were doing and attend services or to engage in private reflection. The two followed the line entering the chapel and sat with the other novices, heads bowed in contemplation as Rabanus led the chorus of voices. They were so happy to be together that it was hard for them to concentrate as each relived the past few hours together secure in the knowledge that they would keep this private life a secret only to be shared by each other.

The rigid, monotonous routine of work, prayer, study, and sleep was designed to make the mind and will submissive to the Lord. For the Benedictines, this meant strict adherence to the Book of the Hours, the main prayer book. It was divided into eight sections, or hours, meant to be read at specific times of the day. The readings were prayers, psalms, hymns, and others aimed at promoting salvation.

Chapter Seven

This Vespers service was followed by a dinner of bread, meat, and ale, eaten in silence, and following this they retired to their cells where Compline was recited before retiring at 6 p.m., the last service of the divine office.

Gilbert was happy to return to her cell. As they undressed and lay down on their straw pallets, they fell into a deep sleep, arms around each other, content with what the day would bring.

At 2 a.m. the bell for Matins was sounded and all the monks and novices woke to the night office recitation. By Lauds, at 5 a.m., the early morning service was attended by all again in the larger hall, followed by more bread and drink, then by Prime, which Rabanus presided over. Silence reigned from Compline to Lauds, so there was some murmuring as the monks prepared to speak the words in the recitation.

Thomas came over to the two after Prime and said, "Rabanus has made his assignments for you both. First you are to go to the barber and be shaved, faces and tonsures, although you both clearly do not need the shave as yet. Then Gilbert should go to the scribe room where they will assign you your tasks."

Elated, Gilbert said, "I will be in the scribe room?" She was most anxious to serve in that way and have access to all the manuscripts in the archives of the library.

"To be seen," said Thomas. "You will start there and they will assign you further depending on your skills. They are also responsible for the education of the novices and boys from the village. Which tasks you will do is to be found out."

"Henricus, you are to report to the cellarer who provides provisions for the monastery. He needs a helper with number skills, someone more, uh, literate than himself."

They quickly made their way to the barber and had the circle shaved from the top of their heads, a small circular covering placed over the spot. Then off went Henricus one way and Gilbert another, to be separate until the next time they could return to their cell.

They could have been assigned to a number of different positions, but this was the one that pleased Gilbert the most. She did not want to wash clothes or cook as she had to do those chores in Mainz for her family; nor did she want to raise vegetables and grain, to reap, sow, plough, thatch, or haymake. She knew that monks were not so particular about what they did to serve, but her primary intent in coming here was to study. She was sorry Henricus could not be assigned with her, but she knew that she was more advanced in her studies than he.

This is most wonderful, thought Gilbert, not wanting to upset Henricus with her assignment. He, most in tuned to her now, said, "That is where you should be. Go. I will be fine. We will be fine. I will see you at Vespers. At least I did not get assigned to the almoner giving out alms to the poor again, or to the wine and ale producer. At least they recognized some of my skills." He walked away not daring to look back lest someone see him staring at his loved one.

By the time he got to the cellarer, the old monk in charge was surrounded by piles of grain and other provisions, hanging meat drying on hooks, and other barrels containing the vegetables and raw foodstuffs used in cooking. Gustav, the monk, was getting on in years, and had trouble with his back and eyesight, hence the infusion of new blood into the cellar to help with the organization and meting out of nourishment.

Henricus nodded as he walked in, unsure if he was to speak or not. Gustav looked up at him, unaware at first that there was anyone standing there until he practically tripped over Henricus's sandaled feet.

"Yes," said Gustav.

Chapter Seven

"I am Henricus, newly assigned to aid you."

"Who?" asked Gustav.

Henricus repeated what he said, louder this time because he assumed Gustav was a little deaf.

"Oh yes. They told me something about that; was it today? Yesterday? No matter." He started to walk away to the disorder of the provisions when Henricus walked up to him again and said, "What would you like for me to do to help you?"

"Oh. Are you here to help me?" They started the conversation over again. Henricus now knew why he had been assigned here. Gustav was clearly getting on in years and could not function as the cellarer much longer. As a result, of late, there were foodstuffs gone to waste because he used the newly picked provisions before using the older ones that were left to rot in their containers.

Henricus pushed up his sleeves and told Gustav, "Sit down here on this cask and tell me what needs to be done today. I will do the lifting and organizing if you tell me what you want." In reality, Henricus already had a plan devised spontaneously as he looked around to date each barrel as it was filled and mark it with the provision inside, sorting them by type. He also rearranged the hanging meat so that they would send the older ones to the cook first, the newer ones arranged in the order they were hung.

By the time the bell for Terce rang at 9 a.m., he had moved almost all the provisions into a new order of distribution. Stopping what he was doing, both he and Gustav recited the Little Hour of divine office before returning to the task at hand. They had three hours to Sext at noon before their work would be interrupted by the call to prayer and reflection. He found some paper and made a chart of the provisions on hand and those that were needed. *I will write a note to indicate to the farm workers what they need to replenish. That should fill in the stores nicely,* he thought.

While Henricus was reforming the cellarer's role, Gilbert reported to the Sacrist, who barely looked up at her from the manuscripts he was sorting to be distributed to the sixty or so scribes working in the library. The smell of parchment, ink, and books was so pleasing to Gilbert's nose and eyes that she looked at the Sacrist and smiled.

He looked up at her unexpectedly and said, "What pleases you so, child?"

"The manuscripts," she said in as low a voice as she could muster, wiping the smile off her face.

"And why is that?" he asked.

"I want to read them all."

"All, but to do that you have to have Latin and Greek!" He snorted.

"My Latin is fluent, my Greek less so, though enough to get by."

"Really," he said handing her a text in Latin and asking her to read. She did so flawlessly. "But do you know what you have read?" he asked.

"It is a tract on commerce in ancient times. A religious parable about how money is the source of quarrel and misunderstanding and . . ."

"Enough. Try this," he said handing her a Greek passage he had just sorted through on his enormous table.

"Translate as you go along," he told her sternly.

She did. Then Gilbert told him again, "My Greek is less well developed, but I am a fast learner. I do understand this nevertheless. Do you want me to tell you what it . . ."

"No. Can you scribe as well and illuminate?"

"Scribe, yes. I am less well endowed with the art of drawing. But the novice I came with is a master at picturing."

"And who is this and where is he?" asked the Sacrist.

Chapter Seven

"I believe he was assigned to the cellarer. We just came here yesterday from Mainz and were assigned today to our respective tasks."

"I see. You are useful. I will start you on this. There is an empty table in the back with ink and quill, and when you are done pass it on to one of the illuminators. You will also be assigned to teach a class of local boys from the village. Every day in the morning do that, and then report to me by Sext. That is all. Someone will bring you the pages to transcribe." With that he turned away and went back to the table of papers in front of him.

Gilbert wanted to ask if she could read other manuscripts shelved in their library but thought that this interaction had gone far enough and she would wait until he saw her work. Making her way to the empty table in the back, she sat on a stool, opened the drawer, and took out the ink and quill. Soon, someone brought the parchment she was to copy and the paper and blotter to use as she went. Carefully she spread the work in front of her, read through so as to get an idea of the content, and then carefully wrapped her small fingers around the quill, dipped it in the ink, and began what for her was not work but a pleasure. She was a scribe, at least for part of the day, and access to this treasure of books was within her reach.

She worked steadily until Sext, prayed with the others, then returned to the table to continue. She finished before the others and looked around. It was an hour before Nones and she had completed all the work given to her. An older scribe in charge of the workload came over to collect her papers. He looked them over carefully, looked up at her, and said, "Well done. You finished neatly, correctly, and quickly. Good traits in a scribe."

"May I go ahead and read until Nones?" she asked.

"Yes. But make sure you put the parchments and books back

exactly from whence you have taken them. There is an order here that must be maintained. You may read until prayer time. The Sacrist will inspect your work too."

Gilbert stood, went over to the library rooms, and selected a text. Sitting on the floor, she read until the bell rang for prayer, then carefully returned the book to the shelf. She wanted to talk to someone about what she had read, but now was not the time.

After Nones, the monks all went back to their cells to prepare for Vespers and rest after a long day. She got there as Henricus was entering, and once inside, they held back vocal enthusiasm and kissed deeply, enjoying the hour before Vespers to be together.

chapter eight

Life in the monastery went on in an endless pattern of prayer, work, and teaching. Henricus, having transformed the cellar into a routine that was organized and efficient, went there less: to oversee the morning's delivery of goods to the kitchen and in the evening to replenish the stock with goods reaped during the day. Old Gustav had less and less to do, so he spent most of the day between prayers sleeping in a corner of the cellar while laying on bags of grain. That was satisfactory to everyone considering his age. At least he felt useful. Henricus was asked to help in the scribe room part of the day as he turned out to be a skilled illuminator, careful and thoughtful of the images he illustrated around the borders of the pages they worked on.

Gilbert taught children in the school, all the while gaining more and more knowledge as she made her way through the library reading the manuscripts that lined the walls. Even Rabanus recognized her talent after having once passed by as she taught the children of the village in such a way that he stayed in the back of the room just to listen to her. He often came up to the scribe room to get a reference for the encyclopedia he was writing only to find that she was reading it.

"Excuse me," he said. "Are you quite through with that?"

She looked up at him while deep in thought about the passage she had just read, recognizing him and standing up as a child caught stealing food. Looking down, she said, "Is this the manuscript you seek?" She held the heavy tomb out in front of her.

"You are reading this on your own time I presume. Do you comprehend the passages fully?"

"Yes. But I have need of clarification,. No, not of the translation, but of the meaning." She thought, *Just ask him your question.*

"I am perplexed by this passage . . .," she went on in detail about what she wanted to ponder further.

Rabanus looked at her, knotted his brows, and then looked around the room at the diligent scribes and illuminators who merely copied text without understanding or questioning the meaning. "You do this after your assignments are complete?"

She nodded, looking downward.

"Come to my study each day when your work scribing is done. Instead of teaching, I want you to help me with my encyclopedia, a most important work I have undertaken. I have need of an assistant, one who can help me organize and transcribe the material both in Greek and Latin. Start tomorrow."

He started to walk away and turned adding, "We can discuss what you want while you are working for me."

Gilbert was delighted with this prospect. Not only would she have access to all the documents in the library, but she would have the ability to have ongoing discussions with this learned man about the content. Excited by this prospect she looked around for Henricus.

Having just entered the library, he was on his way to the table where he was working on a manuscript. She went over and he whispered to her that they had to go to the barber and he needed his first shave.

"Come with me today since I heard that Comenius, the

Chapter Eight

eunuch, is going there and he too needs not a shave. It will be less conspicuous."

She nodded, and when he finished his work, she followed.

Father Comenius was a jovial, rosy cheeked, rotund abbot who always nodded and smiled at the young novices. He worked teaching adults in the village and knew Gilbert as the person who taught the children.

They all met outside the barber's who looked up at them and said, "Ah. The barefaced ones." He gave a snort as he said this.

"Actually, I think I might need your services today," said Henricus touching his lip and chin.

The barber came closer, squinting at his face, and said, "Slightly. Once with the blade should be enough."

"You can see, can you not?" asked Henricus, afraid to let someone with poor eyesight touch his face.

"Enough for this," said the barber. "Sit."

Comenius and Gilbert watched as the barber quickly removed Henricus's moustache and cleaned his chin, followed by a once-over to his pate.

"Next," he said as Comenius sat down. "Just a little, top only," Comenius said.

The barber laughed. "You do not know how lucky you are. Some come here every other day, but you, I rarely see. This one too," he added pointing at Gilbert. "Two peas in a pod I guess," intimating that Gilbert too was a eunuch.

Henricus could hardly suppress his smile. *Let them think what they want. Maybe this is for the best. That way no one will question her*, he thought.

Comenius looked at her and was inwardly delighted to find yet another like him among the monks. He had not thought of it before, but now that the barber mentioned it, he took in the idea completely.

While the monks had taken vows, including silence, in practice their encounters were frequent and extended. Comenius became a regular part of their lives, conversing in whispers and giving Gilbert advice and news of any slight infraction by any of the other monks. He flitted from one encounter to the next, into everyone's business. This he brought back to her whenever he could find her. *He gossips like a woman*, she thought.

While Gilbert was very busy with Rabanus and her other duties, she knew this ruse would be helpful so she did not so much as encourage him as lend an ear whenever he wanted. He would often now knock on their door, waiting for one of them to admit him so they may pray together and he could deliver news of who did what to whom and when. They had to take care he did not enter until they were fully clothed.

Gilbert worked almost exclusively for Rabanus over the next months, carefully cataloguing what he needed to include in the encyclopedia he was working on, and transcribing his notes and prodigious output of poetry and verse. Always grateful to find someone so literate to help him, he would make time for her questions, delighted that someone of her caliber was a member of this monastery.

"You have a quick brain," he said, adding that he wanted her to read this or that, hone her Greek so she was more literate in some document he needed to translate. He relied on her more and more, confiding in her any thoughts he had about the running of the monastery or some innovation he wanted to implement.

"My goal is to make this place the Alexandria of our land. I know I am to be more pious and that our purpose is to educate the heathens, but this is my life work, what I will be remembered for.

Chapter Eight

Without your help, it would take much longer," Rabanus sincerely said complimenting her.

She became his secretary and spent hours searching out documents in the library that he could use, while supervising the scribes who transferred the writings to a larger encyclopedia of the world, as it was known. All the while, she read through the library's documents, systematically absorbing as much as she could, managing Rabanus's work with greater and greater skill.

The head scribe, naturally, was jealous of her productivity. *If anyone should be his aide, it should be me*, he thought. He made it more and more difficult for her to deal with him, often not helping her locate a manuscript or accusing her of misplacing it when she returned some text. When he went to Rabanus to complain, he was rebuffed with, "I need Gilbert's help. I expect you to cooperate completely." With that, Rabanus waved him away.

It is not a good thing to have enemies in a monastery, especially when you are hiding a monumental secret. Whether a man or a woman, jealousy of favor by the king or abbot was cause for concern.

One night she discussed this with Henricus who noticed a change in the head scribe when Gilbert entered the library.

"You must be more cautious. We have been here for a while now and have become lax with the ease we have fooled them into accepting you. But we should be as vigilant as ever. It is wonderful being with you in our private moments and at night, but during the day we have to be careful that no one suspects anything is amiss. No talking about anything personal during the day," said Henricus.

"Yes. You are right. But most of the time I just do not attend to it at all. I am so busy with the work that I do not even notice. The work is so important," she said trailing off, lost in another world he was not a part of.

"And to continue, you must be more careful of who is watching and what you are doing," Henricus said.

"I know you are trying to protect me. I love you more for that. Am I not walking and talking as a man? Am I not keeping to myself enough? What is it that you see? Tell me," she said her hands up in the air.

"That for instance. Men do not talk with their hands gesturing as much. Take care about that, and sometimes your voice rises too much. They are used to Comenius's pitch, but not yours."

"Rabanus does not even look at me when I speak. He answers without a gaze, his nose in some text or dealing with the abbey workings. But I have noticed his aide looking at me often. I will take care, Henricus."

"I know you will. I adore you more for being able to talk to you so. Now, let us pray Matins."

After prayers, they removed their clothing and lay on the straw pallet, arms entwined in a lover's embrace.

Chapter Nine

Gilbert seemed to have made two enemies without even trying. Her inattention to anything except her work was an impediment to keeping herself safe from prying eyes and ears. The head of the library was insanely jealous of his domain. Gilbert was constantly in and out of the library doing research and checking on the progress of some tract or other. The monk, the head scribe, stared and glared at her. Gilbert should have been self-conscious about being watched. But she was so absorbed in her work that she paid little attention, except when she needed him to direct her to some manuscript necessary to complete a section for the encyclopedia she and Rabanus were working on.

Henricus, if he was at his desk, would use those times to come up to the monk and ask him something to distract him from her. This most often worked, but, if Henricus was working in the cellar, she was not protected from the snide remarks such as, "You are not taking enough care with these manuscripts," or "You put the last one back on the wrong shelf." Or worse, "You are a newcomer. Who gives you the license to be Rabanus's helper?" This he mumbled under his breath. Gilbert was sure she never misplaced the pages, but. rather than argue with him, she held her tongue and said, "I will try to be more careful in the future."

Rabanus's aide was jealous of her closeness with the abbot that he seemed not to be able to duplicate. It was his job to help run the estate, to make sure tasks were done and decisions carried out, and to keep the books on the costs and expenses of the abbey. But he never became Rabanus's confidant or shared in the intimacy that Rabanus and Gilbert shared as they argued some point of faith or information clarity. Often Rabanus asked Gilbert what she thought about some decision concerning the abbey lands, and to avoid the ire of the aide, Gilbert would say, "I do not know anything about the running of an estate so I do not venture to give you any advice." He would persist, and she would lower her voice and tell him her thoughts only if the aide was off somewhere out of range of overhearing the conversation.

The work was going well, and they had completed more since she started helping him than he had finished previously. Gilbert's knowledge had grown and her facility with Latin and Greek translations was perfected. Always she wanted to learn more, and her questions to Rabanus flowed freely. Their discussions were lively and animated as they argued some point of theory and practice.

"The only place better for your education would be Greece," Rabanus said one day.

"Why is that?" she asked.

"The libraries there connected with the Church are enormous and your facility with Greek would provide access to a whole new area of study. That is the next library you should read through. It would also give you the opportunity to work on a project of your own, one that you initiate and can complete in your lifetime. But do not fear, I am not sending you away. I take great pleasure in our discussions and would not like you to go anywhere until our work is complete."

"Yes. I would like to have access to their compendium. But not until our work is finished."

Chapter Nine

"This work will not be completed until my demise. It is ongoing. The new becomes the old as soon as the day is over. Or until the Lord takes me."

"That is a long way off," Gilbert replied.

"If God is willing," Rabanus answered, turning back to his work.

That evening Comenius knocked on their door to tell them the latest news of the abbey. He often fetched them before dinner. Talkative as ever and finding Henricus not yet back from the cellar where there was some crisis or other concerning rats in the grain, he sat down on the single stool and animatedly talked to Gilbert.

"Then, the barber nicked the cheek of one of the monks who lashed out at him and started a verbal attack that was so loud that everyone came running to see who was using profanities in the abbey. Everyone stood at the door and finally one of them pulled the monk away who by now had his hands on the throat of the barber and was about to cut him with his own razor."

"He did not, I hope," said Gilbert.

"No. Of course not, but. he did frighten him. I would not want to be the next person the barber works on. His hands trembled so."

Comenius laughed holding his hands around his big belly.

Gilbert smiled at him. Comenius stared and said, "You know. You remind me of someone."

"Who is it?" she asked wary that he might suspect something about her demeanor. She rarely smiled or laughed outside the confines of the cell.

Comenius, lost in remembrance, said, "Do you know how I came to be here? You have never asked. I did not come willingly as you did. I was condemned to this life. Forced here because there was nowhere else for me to be," he said as tears welled.

"Do not tell me if it makes you sad," she said trying to console him.

"I want to tell you. It is between you and me since I feel a kinship."

Gilbert, not knowing what to do, decided to let him tell his tale if that was what he wanted, but. she certainly was not willing to tell hers to the abbey gossip. She nodded for him to proceed.

"I was a young man, thirteen, and in love with a girl from my village. She granted me her affection even though she was not yet twelve and we were not married, and unfortunately her father caught us in the hayfield. He dragged me into the village where, for my transgression, I was castrated. Not completely you understand, just like the bulls, but. enough to render me unable to procreate and to stunt my development and maturity. Then, they sent me to the abbey so I could no longer see or hear from the girl or cohabit with any other. Everyone in the village knew and I was shunned, so I went willingly. It was not a call from the heavens that brought me here, but a sin."

"For which you have atoned," said Gilbert.

"Yes. But it is difficult. I had no desire. You understand I assume, although you are younger than I. But that is your future."

He, like the barber, assumed that Gilbert was a eunuch too since she was beardless and small boned. She and Henricus decided to let this fallacy persist because it helped disguise their secret.

He moved his stool closer to her. "Can I tell you a secret?"

"If you like," she said not wanting him to say anything he did not want.

"As you know, I teach the adults in the village. Well, there is a new family and the couple is as yet childless, and they both came for instruction and today. And . . ."

Chapter Nine

"Yes," said Gilbert as Comenius hesitated for some moments before continuing.

"I, for the first time in many years, being not only celibate. But unable to be aroused, suddenly," he looked at her with wide eyes, "found myself erect. I did not know I was able. My surprise forced me to end the class early, and I do not know what to do. I have been thinking about it all day, and whether this is possible. How did this occur? Is there somewhere to go or ask to see what is going on? How has this happened to me?"

Gilbert, a surprised look on her face, of course knew nothing of this, or how it was possible. She did not know that some eunuchs were capable of this, or that in history there were eunuch lovers who ensured that women of royalty would not be with child as a result of their affections.

"I do not know. I know that monks are to be celibate, but I do know that some leave their cells to go to others after the day is done. I do know that it is not allowed in our belief. This is different. I think that for the first time since you have come here, you need to control your impulses and not tell anyone else of your dilemma. You must learn to be celibate now. You must learn to be as pious as possible if you are to remain here," she said.

"Yes. You are right. You are wise, young one. But . . ." he looked up and smiled, his eyes sparkling, "she really was beautiful."

The Vespers bell rang and it was time to go to dinner.

"Come, let us go. Put those thoughts out of your head and know I will pray for you to resolve this," Gilbert said, standing, opening the door, and joining the others as they filed out of their cells.

"I will be tested the next time she comes to class," he said as they joined the procession.

Henricus already was in the hall waiting for her. She walked over, Comenius following, and Henricus whispered, "I waited for you to be seated. Comenius again? It is every day now that he comes to our cell. He is always with us when we are not working."

"Are you jealous?" Gilbert said in jest.

"No. Just envious of the time that could have been mine."

"I will make it up to you later. I promise. His talk has made me ever more grateful of our closeness."

Comenius was off talking to some other monks. But. they reserved a seat for him. Eventually he came over and sat down. He chatted easily when there was to be silence, the others trying to silence him with their eyes and fingers held up to their lips indicating quiet.

Rabanus began the prayers and all the monks prayed silently. Comenius, at last quiet, could not keep his good fortune to himself. By the time he sat down, he had told his intimates, the few other monks who he knew would be sympathetic, of his current state. He would later garnish opinion from as many as he could of how to handle his new state and what he should do about the female who had awakened his desire.

Rabanus, particularly happy with Gilbert's work that day, asked that she come up to the front of the room and lead one of the prayers. No one else not in the inner circle of the abbey had ever been called to the front. The monk from the library and the monk who was his aide, who sat on either side of him at dinner, fumed, knotting their brows, knuckles white with anger. No one else noticed, but their eyes met as each gritted their teeth when Gilbert made her way to the front to read.

Chapter Ten

There comes a time when all good things end. It may be purposeful, or it may just be the succession of time that transcends the bliss that Gilbert and Henricus found in the routine of the days at the abbey. Departure was not their intention even though Gilbert had a yearning to see the great libraries of other lands and to study in the musty corridors of learning, conversing with others who shared her passion for enlightenment. Henricus could have stayed here in their circumstances for the rest of their natural lives, happy to be with her and not very mindful that somewhere else they could survive and perhaps bear offspring. They lived for the moments they shared and the life that became their routine. Each thrived in their own way, she in her growing capacity to read and understand even the most esoteric texts; he in his contentment with being the most talented illuminator in the scribe room.

Her status in the abbey grew as Rabanus put her in positions of authority by proxy. Other monks came to her before presenting Rabanus with their ideas and she offered her opinion sparingly trying not to anger his aide who should have been the one they consulted. The aide, Wygard, was a small man with hunched shoulders and a hooked nose, older than Rabanus, whose ego was bruised easily and for which he fought back with words and action when he found the chance. He held grudges and looked for any opportunity to strike back at the helpless victims by assigning them the worst tasks at the abbey or gathering evidence to have them punished.

One day, upon overhearing two of the monks talking in the open in the cloister through an open window, he had the opportunity to vent his wrath. The covered walkway surrounded the quadrangle, a colonnade on the outside, windows on the inner side. They happened to walk near the one where the aide could listen.

"I have been caught before. I cannot meet you later. We are being watched. I do not want to spend another term in isolation," said Hertwig.

"Don't fear. We can meet in the field after the others have left. There is cover near the trees on the far edge and everyone else will have left after a day of planting," Girlach replied.

"I certainly want to," said the first as he reached a hand toward the other to caress his face.

They looked around and, seeing no one near, kissed in the shadow of the overhang, and then parted.

All this Wygard listened to and witnessed and plotted their capture and punishment. Not that he was free of sin. Not that he followed all the rules exactly as proscribed. But here was an opportunity to bring the sinners to the attention of Rabanus and raise his level of esteem in Rabanus's venerable eyes. *It is my duty to tell what they are about. I will find them in the act and expose them. Hertwig must be the instigator and he has been warned before. It is the lash for him for sure. I will make that happen,* he thought.

That afternoon as the sun started to set, Wygard and another monk found the two men in a sexual perversion, a sadistic embrace, with Gerlach tied to a tree and being violated by the other. Wygard called out and instructed them, "Cease and follow me back to the abbey." Surprised and embarrassed, they tried to cover their bodies. Without clothing, they were marched to the center of the cloister,

Chapter Ten

put down on their knees, hands in supplication, looking penitent and frightened and shivering in the cold evening air.

Rabanus and the other monks entered the yard at the beckoning of Wygard. He looked down at the two, recognizing that this was an instance where severe punishment was warranted. "You two will be taken to the misericord immediately after being disciplined here. First, you will be beaten with lashes while lying on the ground and the others may step atop you on their way to the Chapter House. No one is to speak to either of you. You will be given a hair shirt this evening, and then both of you will be taken to isolated cells for a length of time that I will determine depending on how penitent you are. You will eat, sleep, and pray separately from the community of your brothers and from each other." He turned to the others assembled. "No one is to talk to these two. They are exiled." He turned around and walked away as the lashing began.

Wygard followed, and Rabanus turned to him and said, "Next time you discover something of this sort, come and tell me first before you act."

Wygard was stunned. It was the duty of the monks to self-regulate and, if that was not the case, to bring infractions to light. That is what he did. But it was also their duty to tell their superior, in this case Rabanus, before taking it upon themselves to act. Wygard had acted without his counsel and forced Rabanus to inflict the highest level of punishment that he had in his power. He did not like to do this, nor did he care to be burdened with jealousy and revenge among his charges.

No monk likes to be so isolated. Monasteries are communal places and this punishment, in a community where the collective work of the monks was encouraged, was like a minor excommunication from their life work. Comenius watched in horror. He knew this could be his fate if he proceeded with his desire for the woman in the village. Shuddering, he moved closer to Gilbert and Henricus who looked on with fright. *What would happen to us,* Henricus thought, *if we were found out?* He watched the lash come down on the backs of the two men as the welts turned to bloody streaks on their backs. The men stood frozen to the spot. When the lashings ended, they were left on the ground as each monk in turn walked across their backs and then on to evening prayer and dinner. The two penitents were led away to their cells, to be locked in alone for an undetermined time without contact with the others.

Silence permeated the service and dinner, and it extended to the slow walk back to their cells for the evening. Comenius stayed close to Gilbert and Henricus throughout the night, going back to his own cell reluctantly only at Gilbert's urging.

"Go now," Gilbert prodded. "It will be time for prayer soon. We will wait for you on the night stair to go down. But if you do not sleep, your judgment will be all the poorer."

"Yes. You are correct. But Gilbert, I am weak and this may be difficult to get over. I am not sure if I really want to after all. Remember, I am not as pious as you two are."

Henricus, anxious for him to leave them, at last said, "People are as pious as they wish. Their hearts are not known by anyone. It is keeping up the appearance that lets you remain here. That is what you should work on. And take care that when you see her again in your classes that you are not outwardly showing too much affection for her. Go and rest Comenius. Tomorrow will come soon enough and we all need to contemplate our future."

As Comenius opened the door, he turned back to Gilbert who nodded for him to leave.

Once the door was closed, Henricus said, "You see the anger that Wygard holds inside of him. He is very dangerous for us.

Chapter Ten

Vigilance is now the order and we have to be prepared for his stealth. He may not discover our secret. But. he may find some other thing to get to you and cause a rift with Rabanus."

"Yes; the same for the one in the scriptorium. When you are not there to distract him, he is increasingly argumentative and jealous of my work with Rabanus. It is hard to tell his moods. I try to stay away from him as much as I can, but he is the gatekeeper for the work we are doing. Rabanus's output is very great, and I am constantly in the room where he oversees everything concerning the library."

"That is his domain. He watches everything. With any little mistake, he flies into a rage and makes the scribe begin again, no matter how long it took quill to paper to get as far as they did. He tears it up and has them start over. He tolerates no errors, which is as it should be, but he takes it to extremes. I am lucky he appreciates my scribbles as I create the illustrations for the books, but you can never be sure of him," Henricus noted.

"This place is full of contradictions. We follow the rules, but there are many exceptions. We talk when we are not to, we are chaste in public but not in private, and we are devout as suits our needs and higher purpose. Even Rabanus wants to leave a great work so he will be remembered, but his wish is against the collective mission of the monastery that one should not be more important than another."

"I think what has to be is that you and I prepare for the inevitable. That we put in place a means of leaving that brings us to another location where we can work and live in peace. Maybe there is a place not as renowned as this, but nevertheless, one that gives us safety and protection from those who would have us undone."

"Where do you have in mind that such a thing is possible?"

"I think I should like to take you to Greece where there is more for you to learn and where I can watch you flourish. That is my wish."

"What do you or I know about Greece except that there is a library there? It is very far away, much longer than just a few days walking. How could we, penniless monks, possibly get there from here?"

"I will find out. I heard there is a villager who came from Greece. I will talk to him generally about it next time I see him. We will find a way, Gilbert."

"Sleep, Henricus. Comenius will be waiting for us soon. If we keep him too long, he will be looking for us, and I want time to uncouple from you before he opens our door."

"Poor Comenius. His problems are so large to him. He does not have two senior monks trying to undo him. He only sees what relates to him. How did we entangle our life so completely with his?"

"I do not know. I think we just are too easily open and available to his needs. He tells others also, but we are the ones he regards with such closeness."

As they lay sleeping, Wygard stayed awake, reliving the day's happenings and his bewilderment that Rabanus was not lauding his efforts. The real target for him was Gilbert, the upstart, who took over a place where he should have been selected. He would have to create another ploy, a way to get directly to her. He did not say *her* to himself though. He regarded Gilbert as a young novice of special talent who was chosen to be an intimate of Rabanus. The real secret of her existence was even beyond his comprehension. Armed with that knowledge, who knows what would be her fate.

Rabanus did not sleep well either. He did not like to exact such punishment on his monks. But. sometimes they had to be held

Chapter Ten

in check. To be frightened of what could and did occur, although rarely. Sodomy was not allowed. This was not a minor infraction of the rules. Others were at fault. They fell asleep during services, sang the wrong words in church, or broke or ruined property, even keeping some objects for themselves. When found out, their punishment was doled out properly. He pardoned them for first offenses and told them to pray for guidance and support from God who sees all and knows men's hearts. Repeated offenders, those not confessed, were different. No monitoring here. There were a few in misericord who had been there for months, years for one, who never repented. He did not like to do this, but order must be maintained and rules followed for this abbey and its property to remain and flourish.

Sleepless, he rose before Matins to lead the flock who would be very wary today. He went to the sacristy, put on his vestments, and waited in prayer for the monks to arrive through the night stair and be seated.

chapter eleven

For Henricus and Gilbert, it was not easy to plan what to do next. For the most part, they were happy in their enclave of monks, and they distressed over leaving what they considered a safe place. Although they considered it was possible to keep their charade quiet, the clashes of personality and jealousy were becoming more and more apparent and directed specifically at Gilbert; therefore, they were very wary. That was the danger they faced.

Wygard constantly interrupted her work with Rabanus, coming into his office to tell him something about the goings on in the abbey or in the community surrounding. When no one was in the room, he would shuffle papers and move them out of order anticipating that Rabanus would blame Gilbert for some mishap that would slow down their work.

"The history we are working on of Pippin. Where is it?" Rabanus said to Gilbert. "Is it being scribed now?"

"No. It was on this table right here when I finished yesterday. I am sure of it. I will look."

Inevitably she found it in some corner of the room out of place after losing an hour of work time on the next section of the encyclopedia. When she brought it back to the correct place in the office, Rabanus looked at her querulously and asked, "You misplaced it? How unlike you. You need to concentrate. Here, take

Chapter Eleven

this to Meinhard for scribing." He seemed annoyed, and that was what Wygard was after. He wanted to replace Gilbert as the aide, even though she had much more skill and facility with language.

Gilbert carried the handwritten pages out of the inner office and as she passed Wygard's desk, he looked up at her and sneered, having overheard the conversation. Gilbert did not even look at him, but she heard the snort as she closed the outer door.

It was not until she reached the colonnade that she breathed, suddenly aware of the danger he posed. *He went after those two monks with such stealth, what would he do to me and Henricus should he catch wind of our secret? But he won't. We are careful, but he may think of some other scheme and try to get me some other way.* She breathed to calm herself and prepared to face Meinhard and his displeasure. *What is it about these monks who have taken vows? They must always find ways to disturb and deter the mission they have all pledged to uphold.*

She entered the scriptorium at a time when Henricus was in the cellar as the cellarer was getting very feeble and he needed to be there more and more to oversee. Rabanus did not want to replace the cellarer, which gave the elderly monk some status in the abbey. The contented monk often slept in a corner lying on bags of grain and snoring away as Henricus did all the work.

Meinhard was berating some scribe for wasting paper, making too many mistakes, and smudging the border where the illuminator would draw their images. Gilbert waited until his rant subsided, then entered head down, and quietly went to the scribe who was working on Rabanus's special projects. Meinhard saw her out of the corner of his eye. Already angry, he turned toward her and said, "You come to me first. Do not go directly to the scribe. I have told you before." He yelled, "Why don't you follow directions?"

"I am most apologetic," she quietly answered. "I did not want to interrupt you as I am cognizant of your need to keep your scribes on task. I just thought...."

"Do not think here. There is a procedure. Follow it, or I will ban you from entering."

Gilbert knew this was unreasonable, but she held her tongue and merely said, "Yes. I am sorry to bother you with this." Her hands were tucked into her cloak folds, and she stood looking down at the floor, doing everything she could to defuse him. That was something she learned from dealing with her angry stepmother. To answer back only ignited another outrageous barrage of words and action. But Meinhard was not her stepmother. He was a powerful guardian of the library. He might stop her from her personal reading of the rare manuscripts that she still wanted to peruse.

When he had calmed down and sat back at his desk, she said, "Could I please have the completed pages so that Rabanus can review them? It is the work that was completed in the past few days."

He looked up at her, his long nose dripping from his tirade, and stared. She looked down and waited. This was a game of wills and she had to be submissive to this lion waiting to pounce on his prey. He looked back down at the pages that he was reviewing, and after some time, rose slowly and walked over to the same scribe Gilbert had interacted with before. He held out his hand wordlessly and the poor boy gathered the completed work and handed the pages to him without comment. Meinhard did not have to ask. Everyone had heard the conversation between him and Gilbert and shuddered in fear and relief that the object of his fit was not them this time.

Slowly he walked back to his desk, and more slowly held the pages out for Gilbert. She did not take them immediately.

Chapter Eleven

Something inside her made her braver than she was with Wygard, so she stood still looking down at her feet as if she did not see what he held before her. Finally, Meinhard said, "This is what you want. Take them and go."

Gilbert looked up at his eyes, directly staring at them with as little expression on her face as she could muster to indicate her lack of reaction to his scorn. That made Meinhard angrier. "Do you want them or not?" he loudly asked.

A slight smile crossed her face as she took them from his outstretched hand, turned, and walked out the arch and down the stair. Reaching the courtyard, she met Henricus, who was finished with his chores in the cellar and coming up to illuminate some pages for the rest of the workday. Gilbert's smile broadened by the time they met.

"And what pleases you so this fine day?" he asked.

"Just that I survived and I think thrived today. Wygard attacked by misplacing pages in Rabanus's office, and Meinhard vented rage at me that caused no hairs on my head to stand on end. I kept calm in front of both, and that seemed to anger them more, but we have survived another day."

"Merely survived, or thrived. I think what we should be after is for you to thrive. I am increasingly wary that this is the place for you to do that. We will talk later. I do not want Meinhard to be hard on me also. One of us should be in the good graces of the monks."

"I always have Comenius."

They both laughed.

Comenius's day was equally as exciting. He finished his first class of the day, taking over one group of older children, aged nine to eleven, and was rote drilling them in mathematics. Simple counting eluded some of them while others could retain what he taught and would have more skills than the common planters and reapers in the village. Everyone needed to read and recite the prayers, so he spent more time in class with those more adept. The goal was a literate flock that would read scriptures and lead a life commensurate with the church doctrine.

His next class toward the end of the day was for adults. After not coming for two weeks, the woman of his desire, Greta, came and sat down in the second row, looking directly at him. *She is here again. So beautiful. I must be careful not to show my attraction to the others*, he thought.

He began the lesson with a review of the previous lesson, and then he began a new passage of the holy book dealing with an unfaithful wife and her husband. He went over the vocabulary and then had them follow the text he wrote on his slate as he read, each in turn reciting the words. When it was her turn, as with the others, Greta came to the front to recite. He stood next to her as she spoke the words, following them with her finger on the slate. *How wonderful is her shape; her movement is fluid and her stance . . .* He thought all this rather than listened to her so he missed her mistakes that the others had heard. "She makes errors, Teacher," one said, proud of catching the mistakes.

Called back from his reverie by the sound of another voice, Comenius by now was fully aroused under his cloak to his bewilderment. He stood behind Greta until he could bring himself back to some semblance of order, but not before she noticed his ardor and blushed.

The class thought she was reddening because of being corrected by another ignorant student, and she did not dissuade the conclusion because of her kindness to the monk. Everyone knew that monks were not completely celibate, and that there were instances of sexual liaisons with the peasants that were left unspoken. But

Chapter Eleven

Comenius was a eunuch, and this is what confused her and caused her to blush.

When class was over, she stayed behind on the pretext of needing extra help, "If you be so kind, could you please help me with this lesson. There are some things I do not understand."

"Certainly," Comenius said, hurrying the others out until the next time they would meet. "Study your letters and prayers so you may join in at sermons the next time you attend," he called after them. Turning back toward Greta, she looked at him and smiled.

Comenius was a simple man and this was all new to him. Not since he was altered had he felt anything for another human being, let alone a woman. But he did have feelings for Greta. She stirred something in him that he thought was lost forever.

They stood looking at each other, far longer than they should. The peasant women were not shy about sexual favors if it meant more food or some favor that would help in their meager existence. Her curiosity about this monk was what intrigued her and attracted her to his condition. Being practical, she thought, *If I let him touch me, will he give me food?*

Alone in the room, neither of them spoke. She unbuttoned the top of her camisole and her bosom was exposed. Comenius, not able to take his eyes off her breasts, reached out to touch her. She let him, and he bent down to kiss her breasts and touch her face in a caress.

"It is not safe here. Someone will come. We can meet later, or tomorrow. Bring me food. And cloth. We can meet outside the abbey. There is a glen near the water down the road. It is secluded."

Comenius, still staring at her body, agreed. Greta walked out, looked back over her shoulder, and smiled at him. *I have found my benefactor, and what do I need to do to keep him? Nothing I haven't done before*, she thought.

Comenius had to sit and quiet down before he left the room. He was very excited about the next day. When he had calmed down, he left to go back to his cell, stopping by the storeroom where a sleeping cellarer did not see him take some bread, wine, and dried meat.

Chapter Twelve

Comenius was excited as a new day began, and he anticipated seeing Greta in class. He was awake long before Vespers and stayed awake through Prime. Hardly eating, he sat between Gilbert and Henricus, squirming in his seat and whispering to them that today was the day.

Gilbert tried to pay attention, but her mind was on the work to be done for Rabanus that day and keeping her two banes, Meinhard and Wygard, at arm's length. *Perhaps today I will not have to deal with Meinhard*, she thought. *There is enough to keep us busy in the office organizing the next section of the manuscript.*

Comenius kept his chatter to a low whisper, annoying even those who sat opposite in what was supposed to be utter silence. They tolerated the eunuch, but this was extreme even for him.

As soon as the meal and prayers were over, he stood and quickly left to go to the schoolroom where he taught the children. The adult class was later in the day, and he was eager for a sign from Greta that the time for them to meet was soon.

He had secreted the food he carried under his cloak, and he wrapped cloth for Greta around his already ample waist. It did not occur to him that he was taking anything that belonged to the abbey. Rather, he rationalized that the monks were committed to good works and the care of the peasants working on the property, so he felt this was not outside of their mission to care for the poor and ignorant.

He reviewed the previous lesson with the children, took them impatiently through their lesson for the day and then the recitations and number sums, and drilled them in the day's passage from the scriptures. One boy was not paying attention and pulled the hair of the person in front of him. Comenius singled him out and made him stand on one foot, facing the wall at the front of the room, as an example for the others to obey.

Gilbert left after prayers to go to Rabanus's office and passed the desk where Wygard sat. He stared at her, but she kept her eyes down and walked directly to the table, picking up where she had left off the previous day.

Wygard was still irate. He had thought he had done a good thing by exposing and punishing the two monks, but Rabanus berated him anyway. His esteem in the abbot's eye had declined rather than grown, and he had to find a way to reinstate himself to at least the level he had before the incident. Wygard was single-minded. He only really cared for himself and his power at the abbey. He even had illusions of becoming the abbot when Rabanus was too old or left to go elsewhere.

Rabanus, because he had lashed out at Wygard, was more aware of his assistant's inclinations so Wygard had to keep his wrath of Gilbert to himself, waiting patiently to find something this perfect monk did that was a wrong that could be brought to light and punished.

Gilbert and Henricus were well aware of this real threat, and so they were more cautious than ever. The animosity Wygard had toward her unconsciously spilled over to Henricus, so while enjoying and flourishing in their time here in Fulda, they now were planning to move on and find another place where they could continue their work and Gilbert could study.

Gilbert talked to Rabanus about his suggestion that Athens,

Chapter Twelve

Greece, was where she should travel to study at the great libraries in that country.

"Yes. But I would hate to lose your help. We are well underway now and the next section is quite tricky. On the other hand, I would hate to stifle your further education and prevent your rise in the Church. You know that if you continue in your studies that is a real possibility. You are already more learned than any other monk here, save me," Rabanus complimented her as Wygard gripped his quill and broke it listening in on their private conversation.

Yes. Let Gilbert leave. Then I can assume his role. What can I do to make this happen? Perhaps a change of tactic to encourage his departure. Yes. That is what I will do. Help move the project along. Offer to take the work to the library. Supply them with the documents they need, and bring back finished pages. That is what needs to be done to rid me of this obstacle, Wygard thought.

He walked into the inner office and proposed this to Rabanus who agreed and handed Wygard the pages that needed to be scribed and told him to bring back the previous day's work.

Gilbert, engrossed in her task, barely noticed that she no longer would have to be subjected to Meinhard's tyranny as she outlined the next section to be written. She and Rabanus bent over the documents and proceeded to begin the writing for the day.

Wygard entered the scribe room and told Meinhard, "I will be bringing Rabanus's work from now on and retrieving the finished documents."

Henricus overheard this and sighed in relief that at least this part of their interaction with one acrimonious monk was over.

While all this transpired, Comenius dismissed the children who had fieldwork to do and prepared for the adults to come to class for their lessons. He eagerly waited for Greta to come so that he could again glimpse her ample breasts peeking over her bodice.

When the adults filed in to class, he watched anxiously, looking at the doorway repeatedly for a peek at her. The seats were filling, yet she was not among any of those who came for the afternoon. He waited beyond the time to start class thinking that she was just late. She did not appear at all, and the others were now looking at one another wondering why Comenius was not starting their lesson. They had much work to do, and this disrupted their day, but they tolerated it because the monastery was their benefactor and provided grain and shelter for them in a volatile time of famine and disease. They went to service because of this: less a belief for most than an obligation and fear of purgatory if they did not attend and pray with the monks.

By the end of class, Comenius's agitation grew. He dismissed the class and gathered the food he brought, clearing the leaves of paper, collecting the prayer books, and stacking them neatly in a corner for the next day.

He remembered Greta said he should go to the glen near the water to meet her, so in desperation he ran out with the package of bread and dried meat and through the gate down the path toward the open area she had described.

She must be there. She must. I have the cloth. I have the food, yet she eludes me. That beautiful woman, she must be waiting . . . he thought.

He arrived out of breath from running and found the open area that he thought was where she said she would be. But she did not say it would be after class. He had assumed that she would give him some sign and they would leave separately for their rendezvous.

She was not there. He looked all around, distraught. As Greta was nowhere in sight, he thought, *There must be another glen. I have to look around.* He searched the area and finally called out loud, "Greta, where are you?" On the far side of the glen was a lagoon, a

Chapter Twelve

small waterfall, and the mouth of a cave. He knew that often animals hid in places like this, so he approached with caution, trying to be as quiet as possible. As he neared the area, still calling out her name, she suddenly appeared in the cave opening fully unclothed, her hands covering discretely her bosom and sex.

Comenius was speechless. He at first stopped in his tracks because this was the first naked woman he had seen in many years, since his downfall and his castration. She looked at him and beckoned him to approach, a broad smile on her lips and her arms raised out to expose herself to him fully.

He rushed to her, kissed her lips, and put his arms around her body.

"Did you bring the food and clothing?" she asked.

"Yes." He handed her the food package. She tossed it aside saying, "And the cloth?"

"It is wrapped around my waist."

She led him into the cave where he found a bed of leaves spread out on the dirt. She put her hands on his belt, untied it, and let it fall to the ground. Over his head she pulled the black robe and unraveled the cloth at his waist, making him turn around and around as it unwound. Then she raised his undergarment over his head and looked down at his erection.

For the next hour, Comenius was hers, and she did everything to please him. Fully satisfied, the hour came when he would have to return to the abbey for prayers. Without speaking, she helped him dress again in his robes and nodded for him to leave first.

"Will I see you again? Are you coming to class?" he asked, thrilled at his good fortune.

"A few days from now, bring more food, meat, and wine."

"How will I know when to come here?" he asked.

"When I do not come to your lessons."

She dressed quickly. He watched before he hurried back to the abbey contented.

He barely made it back in time for the evening prayers and dinner. Rabanus noted he came in last and looked at him briefly, as Comenius sat next to Gilbert and Henricus.

Barely able to control himself, he waited patiently to tell Gilbert what had happened to him. But after service, Gilbert had to talk to Rabanus about something to do with their work, and Henricus hurried out to escape Comenius's prater.

That evening, as Henricus and Gilbert prepared for bed, they looked out at the stars, lay down on their cots, and enjoyed each other before sleep overtook them. They lay naked in their bliss and did not hear the door creak open as Comenius, late that night, came into their cell to tell them of his good news. In the moonlight, he saw the two, naked and entwined.

Henricus woke first and tried to cover Gilbert, but Comenius had seen her breasts. He gasped and backed up to the wall of the cell, unable to move. She pulled on her undershirt to cover herself and stood next to Henricus, trying to calm Comenius who looked on in fright.

At first he thought she was the devil, a hermaphrodite, a demon sent to punish him. His thoughts took a while to congeal and as understanding came to him, he realized the charade.

Henricus said, "Be calm Comenius. Sit down. Calm yourself. We will explain."

Gilbert came to Comenius and tried to take his arm, but he recoiled, befuddled in his disclosure. She talked to him calmly.

Finally, they were able to explain their circumstance to him. Comenius, calm now, could not utter a word. Finally, he looked away and said, "I think I understand. Yes. I see now."

"Do not expose us, please," said Gilbert. "I only want to learn. I

Chapter Twelve

cannot as a woman. Do you really understand? Can you keep this secret? For a little while. We will be leaving soon."

He nodded.

"Why did you come in here, Comenius?" asked Henricus.

Comenius, remembering why he had interrupted them so late at night, looked at them and said, "Because I lay with Greta, because I wanted to tell you, my friends, what good fortune befell me, to . . ."

They stayed up until the bell rang for prayers, talking. Neither Henricus nor Gilbert thought that Comenius could remain silent and keep their secret.

chapter Thirteen

Gilbert's motivation to be at the abbey was never religious. Such piety was a vehicle to sate her ambitions for herself—to learn and know, to study and analyze the words of the world as far as it could be known.

She felt close to exhausting her ability to study here, becoming bored with Rabanus's work, which she knew would never be completed. An encyclopedia of the known knowledge of the world was impossible and she recognized history was never complete. Who knows what will happen in the future. It is an ever-changing landscape of war and conquering, politics and disease. She realized that all histories were incomplete and often inaccurate based on the perspective of the writer. Rabanus was no exception. His take on the events were infused with the dogma of the Church.

She had read all she wanted in the vast library here: the supporting documents of the Church and the store of manuscripts accumulated over the years. She was anxious to move on, to go to other libraries, to other countries, to Athens as Rabanus had said, where she knew she could go to satisfy her personal ambitions.

When Henricus and Gilbert were finally alone the next afternoon, they planned their departure. Comenius, wrapped up in his own guilty tryst, was introspectively talking and mumbling to himself, absorbed in an egotistical way in his situation. Shocked though he was at knowing that Gilbert was a woman, he was involved in his own subterfuge and was not about to disclose theirs.

Chapter Thirteen

But knowing that his seclusion would not last, that he could not keep quiet once the shock of their deception was over, Henricus and Gilbert felt the immediacy of their next move. Comenius never kept silent for long about anyone or anything, and this was too big a thing for him to keep to himself, even after they left.

Henricus said, "No one will believe him anyway. He talks nonsense most of the time. He is the abbey jester and he plays the role well. Never is he serious about anything or anyone. We should be safe until we depart. You know, walking to Greece is not possible. We have to prepare for a long trip, one that may be aided if we can find a way to cross the sea. I will look at maps today while you need to broach the subject with Rabanus who needs to write letters of conveyance for you," said Henricus.

"Yes, I think that I have to be forthright with him and tell him I want to move on to the libraries of Athens as he described them to me and that they have become part of my desire to further my education. I think that will work. We have to go soon, before Comenius talks," Gilbert said, and Henricus nodded in agreement.

"Think of a reason that I should accompany you. Perhaps because a monk traveling alone is dangerous, and most times they travel in pairs for safety. That would be reasonable. Then we have to arrange for food for the first part of the journey south. That should be no problem since I work in the cellar, but I do not want to steal. I would rather have Rabanus's blessing. Of course they have to replace me since the old cellarer is feebler than ever."

"If Comenius cannot remain quiet today, you need to prepare the supplies and have them at the ready. He could even tell his paramour, and that village girl would not keep quiet if she thought she could profit from selling the knowledge. You know it is imprisonment, only bread and water if we are uncovered. I will tell Rabanus that we want to depart at dawn because of the favorable spring weather."

"So, we are off. Ask him if we can have an ass to aid us in our travels. That should be a reasonable request."

"I will. Let us hasten to our preparations. I want to leave immediately for our own safety, without seeing Comenius again. He will do whatever he wants, but fear of losing his love may stifle his tongue." Gilbert turned and went off to talk to Rabanus, and Henricus went to the cellar to pack foodstuff for the first days of their journey and then to tell the head scribe of his departure. Meinhard was none too pleased that Henricus would not be working further on the manuscripts he was illuminating so he snatched the papers out of Henricus's hand and tossed them to another scribe. Turning his back to Henricus, he muttered, "Go, out of here with you."

Gilbert gingerly entered the workroom where she and Rabanus had labored. He was sitting at his enormous desk sorting through papers for the day's writing. Gilbert went over to him and waited.

Looking up, he said, "We are working on this section today, a tricky part of history to write . . ."

Gilbert waited while he went on and, when there was a pause, she said, "Rabanus. Sir. You have taught me so much. You have given me the gift of reading in the library."

Rabanus answered, "You are the best mind that has ever come here. There is no need to thank me for using you to aid in my life work."

Gilbert looked down, shy at the compliment that Rabanus gave knowing that it was very rare for this scholar to praise anyone. "I have to tell you something. I have decided to move on. I know that living here and working with you is something I can do for the rest of my simple life. It pains me to leave, but it is something I have to

Chapter Thirteen

do, firstly to spread the good work we do here, and to further my education."

Rabanus looked at her and put his hand on her arm. "I understand child. I just did not think it would be so soon. You go with my blessings."

"I would like an introduction to the Church in Athens. That is where I would like to go. I know it is a long, perilous journey, but if I could take another with me I believe it will be safer and we can work on the way. It will take months to get there, so if I may take an old ass for at least part of the journey I will give it to some poor farmer on the way when it tires and can move no longer."

"Yes. There is an ass in the stables you can have. Load it with some provisions." Rabanus looked away and noticed Wygard listening at the door. "Wygard, just come in."

"As you wish," he said staring at Gilbert.

"I assume you heard that Gilbert will be leaving for a journey. You will take over her duties for now along with the everyday tasks assigned. I will get someone to help you. Let us wish him good luck in spreading our work all the way to Athens. Gilbert, tell all about my encyclopedia, and try to send word with a traveler when you have reached your destination. Wygard, go tell Henricus he will be traveling with Gilbert and have someone replace him in the cellar. Make it someone who will leave the poor old cellarer alone and not disturb his old age with nagging." Rabanus said this as an afterthought, just to make sure that Wygard did not have something else malicious to invoke on another unexpecting monk no matter what his age. He was not about to punish the old cellarer for being old and infirm or for not fulfilling his responsibilities.

Wygard nodded, leaving with a smile on his lips. At last Gilbert would be gone and his power restored.

"And the ass? Which one?" asked Gilbert.

"Of course. Take one of your choice. Pass me a parchment and I will write a letter of introduction for you and Henricus. That should give you entry into monasteries on the way and entry at your final destination." He finished and handed it to her.

"Thank you. I will never forget your kindness and the work of this abbey." She turned and went out the door to prepare for the journey and tell Henricus.

Comenius was on his way to class. The children were waiting. He had his provisions for Greta under his cloak and all he could think about was another meeting with her. Gilbert and Henricus were not what he was paying attention to today. He wanted a repeat of yesterday. He finished with the children and rearranged the room for the few adults attending class. Most of them were illiterate and through repetition they orally learned the prayers. Some were hopeless and could not even repeat the verses gone over time after time. Comenius, jovial and patient always, would begin again and again each day. The only thing that kept them there was the bread and ale served in the middle of class.

They walked in slowly, one or two at first, then the stragglers, but no Greta. That meant he was to go see her after class. Her arrangement was that if she did not come to class, he was to go find her in their glen. Rushing through class, he completed the lesson and dismissed them a half hour early. Rushing out and down the path, the sack of food over his shoulder now, he found her at the edge of the water bathing in the pool. He dropped the bag and joined her, tossing his clothes aside.

Comenius, having been transformed into a eunuch at thirteen, wanted the closeness of another to reclaim the feelings he had as a young man. Greta was not prepared to give him what he desired most, intimacy. Instead, he realized that she was doing this for food, to subsist and lessen her labors in the field. Any idea of

Chapter Thirteen

sharing with her what he found out about Gilbert and Henricus was stifled, buried deep in his awareness when all he could think about was Greta's body.

Not knowing that Comenius was so occupied, Gilbert and Henricus hurried to get their meager belongings together and load the ass with a package of dried meat, bread, and bladders of ale to subsist on for the first few days.

They packed the animal and led him out of the stable as quickly as possible, not bothering to say goodbye to anyone. Walking behind the ass, Gilbert turned around to take one more look at the venerable abbey and then looked forward toward the next part of their life together.

Chapter Fourteen

It took the couple two months of traveling southeast through the cold to reach the Bavarian Alps from Fulda. The distance was 150 miles, but the roads were poor and they made slow progress. Along the way, the townsfolk were afraid of the strangers as they had endured the heirs of Louis to wrest the last vestige of land and spoils from their meager stores of food. The peasants risked their lives, and now no one was to be trusted, not even monks.

Their goal was to reach Lucerne by way of Tegern. The practicality of enduring the elements and having little food would have dissuaded others, but Gilbert was determined, and her steadfastness inspired Henricus to keep going.

"I think we have not anticipated the hardship of this trip, Gilbert," he said on one cold day when they had been deprived of food and drank only melted snow to quench their thirst.

Gilbert did not answer. She was wrapped up in her cloak and deep in her own thoughts of the goal that would await them at the end of their quest.

She is amazing, he thought, *and complains not about the trip or the lack of nourishment.*

Finally, she said, catching her breath from the altitude, "We soon will be at Lake Tegernsee. Surely it will afford us some respite from our condition. We can rest there before the trek to Lucerne. I

Chapter Fourteen

am sure we will find someone to take us in, even a poor cloister, to gain our strength to move on."

"Yes, perhaps we can find a boatman who will transport us south across the lake," Henricus said, admiring her tenacity.

"I do not think the lake is that large to warrant a boat crossing, but perhaps there are some monks making leeway there to establish the beliefs. We shall see. We still have to cross over these mountains to get there," she said as she wrapped cloth around her already snow-soaked feet.

Lake Tegernsee borders the frontier of the Swiss cantons. The Bavarian influence and Benedictine infusion were in their infancy, yet there was a small group of monks living there and trying to instill their beliefs.

"Look Henricus," she said as they reached the peak of a snowy mountain overlooking the lake, "it is below. There are huts there. I can see smoke from some rooftops. Come. The altitude impedes our climbing, but this is downhill. We should make it by nightfall."

His spirits lifted by the prospect of food and shelter, Henricus led the way down the icy snow-covered mount. At the end of the slope, they sat exhausted on a rocky crag, looking out at the village.

"Come, let us not tarry too long and freeze when warm soup may be ahead," Henricus said.

"It is beautiful, is it not?"

"Yes, Gilbert, it is, but night will soon be upon us and we should go the last part down now."

As they approached the village, men were headed to their own huts hauling the fish caught during the hard day of fishing in the partially frozen lake. Seeing two men close by, Henricus called out, "Sirs, is there yet a group of monks here? We are Benedictines and seek shelter and food from our brethren."

Eyed suspiciously, the two men motioned to a spot on the other side of the bay where they kept their small canoes. Grunting, they tucked their chins into their woolen cloaks and went on without offering any further assistance.

"Come. It is not much farther."

Gilbert nodded.

They arrived at the small building as a monk was coming out to get fresh water. Dressed similarly to them, he looked up, put down the bucket, and walked closer.

"I thought my eyes were deceiving me. Have they sent you to help us establish an abbey? We surely need you. We are but four and have more work than we can handle just to maintain ourselves."

Henricus approached and said, "We are coming from Fulda and stop here only en route to Lucerne. But we have traveled far and would most appreciate your help so we may regain our strength before going any farther. In exchange, we will do what we can to help you. I am Henricus and this is Gilbert."

"Come, come, and warm yourself by our fire. I am Reginald and I welcome you."

They entered the small hut, one crude room for living with an attached all-purpose room for prayer and meetings. The other three stood as Reginald introduced the guests.

"This is Henricus and the other, Gilbert. They come from Fulda, the great abbey, and are making their way south. This is Primus, Sebastian, and Crimeon."

"Come and sit by the fire. You both must be frigid with the cold. Did you cross over the alps to get here?" asked Sebastian, the portliest of the four.

"Yes, and it has taken us some time. We would like to regain some of our energy here before undertaking the next part of the journey," said Gilbert.

Chapter Fourteen

Primus brought them warm ale and some bread, saying, "Eat. Slowly. You both look famished. Warm yourselves and then tell us about your journey."

Crimeon grunted and said, "You would think they would have sent someone to help us with our tasks, not two scholars from Fulda. That is the abbey where the scribes are. I bet these two have never worked the soil or tried to spread the word to the people."

Henricus looked up ready to refute this, but Gilbert nudged him and her eyes said to be quiet and let him have his say.

"Two more mouths to feed," Crimeon complained.

"We would be very happy to help you for a while, but we are traveling to Athens. We have letters of transport from Rabanus himself and that is the goal of our trek. We are sorry to disappoint you, but we will do what we can while we are here, hopefully not add to your burden. The thaw is coming and Henricus is knowledgeable about planting and crops, while I taught classes and can organize your school for the children so that they can become literate," Gilbert said.

"Rabanus. From the abbot?" Sebastian said, knowing that very few were that close to the renowned scholar.

"Yes, Gilbert was his aide in his great undertaking, the encyclopedia. Important work," Henricus said with inner pride that his Gilbert was so well versed and knowledgeable. "And I was the cellarer at the abbey. We are not without skills you could use."

"Time for evening prayers then. We take turns. Reginald, would you do the honors?"

"Certainly," he responded, reaching for the prayer book.

Gilbert and Henricus took their manuscripts from the folds of their garments and read along with the text. Completed, the four monks cleaned the bowls and pointed to a pile of straw where the two visitors could lie down for the night.

Morning prayers came quickly and the two travelers slept as they had never before, weary from the first leg of their trip. Gilbert went outside to relieve herself and marveled at the sunrise over the lake. It was beautiful, the light glistening over the surrounding snowcapped mountains, a mist of fog hovering over the lake.

Henricus joined her, and they smiled looking out over the miracle of nature. "Amazing," he said, "such wonders in this world and more to see."

Gilbert agreed and said, "We should stay here for some time until the field is sown and they have a chance to see how they can proceed and perhaps have an abbey built here someday."

"We will have to find some time together. We are in too close quarters here inside this hut."

"We can tarry here until it gets a little warmer. We will find a way, Henricus, we always have. I am missing you too."

Where there is a lake, there is fish and silt as the lake rises and falls with the runoff of the mountain as it thaws. After prayers, Henricus grabbed a hoe and went out back and started to break up the winter frost and unearth fertile soils to plant crops. The four monks went about their tasks noticing his efforts yet saying nothing. He found some potatoes and cut them to plant, and found some seeds as he made his way through the field.

Gilbert took her bible and walked through the small village, coming back with three children who she promised to tell stories of amazement. She sat them down in the noon sun on some logs and told them bible stories.

By midafternoon they came in for some ale and bread that was laid out on the table for them. Henricus's hands were blistered and raw, and Gilbert wrapped them in a salve she made from herbs she brought with her.

Chapter Fourteen

"I will help you tomorrow," said Sebastian. "Together we will finish the field faster."

"I will too," said Primus, "and Crimeon too. Am I correct in volunteering you?"

"Yes," he nodded looking down at his feet while his hand was clenched in a fist. Crimeon did not like being told what to do.

Henricus vowed to work on him. He was used to monks harboring thoughts and actions contrary to their mission.

"Sebastian, you can come with me tomorrow and gather up more children for bible study. If we can get them to come, it follows that the parents may find some time. Literacy is important. It opens the world to wonder," Gilbert said.

"So you are staying?" Sebastian asked.

"For a while," Henricus said.

The six monks turned their attention to evening prayers while Henricus and Gilbert said a silent prayer that they would be successful here and return to their journey.

Chapter Fifteen

Their sojourn on the shores of Lake Tegernsee was uneventful and certainly did not advance Gilbert's quest for knowledge. There were no texts to read and discuss, and these monks were consumed with the rudiments of daily life, unable to contemplate anything beyond their labors. Gilbert went about her daily chores, then taught the children of the village most of the afternoon. Meanwhile Henricus helped in the planting and the designing of an ampler edifice that the monks were foreseeing as part of their future there. Their grandiose plans for a major abbey had to be put on hold while they struggled just to provide guidance and nurturance for themselves and the people of the village.

The four other monks, Reginald in particular, were kind and tolerant. They prayed daily together, and Sebastian worked diligently following Henricus's lead in a planting scheme that would maximize the land around their small enclave.

"This is the way it is at Fulda," Henricus told them. "They organize the planting and rotate the crops to ensure a constant supply during the good weather. Then they store all the grain and dry the herbs so as to have a reserve in winter. Gilbert can show you which herbs to pick for cooking and which to dry for other uses, including herbal teas for ailments. You need to build a dry storeroom to do this, and a larder that can serve you while you continue to build

Chapter Fifteen

here. It can be expanded later to supply a larger number of monks once you are firmly established and grow."

"I see," said Sebastian, "come and let us begin the expanded garden. I am sure the villagers will aid if we share the crops with them in exchange for their labors."

"That is exactly what the larger abbeys do. They manage the crops, planting, and exchanges between the people surrounding the abbey and themselves. In exchange they also provide protection, but that is in the future when you grow larger in number," said Henricus.

"I will go to them now and explain. Even the women can help once a larger portion of the ground is cleared. They can plant the seeds in the furrows, and the children can help," Primus added.

All except Crimeon were pleased in their new found helpers. His ideas for the abbey to be were discarded, and this threatened him. Although the monks were communal and focused on charity and spreading the word of the lord, power became a corruptible force even within this small group of practitioners.

"The ground here is not level. It rises up the mountains that surround, and the lake often overflows its banks and drowns out the plantings. Did you think of that in your grand scheme, Henricus?"

"On our journeys we have seen plantings along the sides of mountains. With a hoe, those successful have created rows perpendicular to the mountain and tiered the planting along the contours of the slope. This works very well for certain crops, and is easily expanded so as to avoid the water line. We can use our ass to help with the furrowing."

Crimeon just grunted.

"It is worth trying. Come Gilbert, let us walk through the village people and see if we can arouse interest in this project. You know them even better than I since you teach. I assume the rest of us are in agreement?" said Reginald, the kindest of the four, his eyes lingering at Crimeon's stare.

The rest stood and walked out of the small shelter to begin work.

"Why is he so gruff with Henricus? His dissatisfaction is so obvious to all," asked Gilbert as they walked away.

"It is his way. He likes to have others follow his lead and is suspicious of those who do not follow. That is all right for the rest of us, but since your arrival, he recognizes that you have knowledge that he cannot hope to have based on your experiences in Fulda. I hate to say it but he is jealous, even with his vows, he remains a person you have to walk about softly."

Gilbert nodded and said, "You are the peacemaker here. I have encountered this desire for control before. It is partly the reason we left Fulda. Only Rabanus protected me from goings on of the head scribe and his assistant. I can see we will stay here only a short time. We must be going, but only after this project is underway and you are prepared to continue on your own."

"I know your desire to be on your journey. When you are ready to go I will miss you both. So will the children. But I understand your mission and can only say the Lord is leading you and will watch over you on your journey."

For the next two months Gilbert and Henricus transformed this small place into a working farm with the village people's support. They all worked for a mutual goal, to sustain them in the winter and make the area grow into a more formidable sanctuary and focus of the town.

One day in mid-spring, she and Henricus took a walk along the bank of the river.

"I think it is time to leave here and move on."

Chapter Fifteen

Henricus nodded, "Yes, they are well on the way to full planting and I believe you have exhausted your supply of texts to read. With no one to discuss your many questions you must be anxious to leave."

"Yes. I think Crimeon was staring at my earlobe. There is a small mark where my piercing was and clearly men do not have this. Before he gets too curious we should go. Also I miss being alone with you."

"There is little privacy anywhere in this place. Let us tell them after dinner. We can leave tomorrow. There is little to keep us here. I am sure they will give us some provisions for the next part of our journey to Lucerne. It is far, but the weather should not impede our progress."

That evening they told the four they were departing the next day. After dinner, Reginald packed a cloth with enough food and provisions for a few days, as much as they could spare until the crops came in. In the morning, after the early prayers, he accompanied them out of the village as they made their way around the lake and headed southwest.

"Be safe my brothers."

"And you be prosperous in your planting and building efforts," said Henricus.

The two travelers resumed their travels and did not look back. Their future was ahead.

Henricus was in charge of their route, but this time Gilbert wanted information about the journey.

"We are headed southwest, are we not Henricus?" she said as they skirted around the lake.

"Yes, we have to get to a place where we can take another form of transportation. We cannot possibly walk all the way on foot, riding alternatively on the animal. So this part of the journey strays a little to the west, to Lucerne, then to Aventicum where we should be able to find a boat for part of the journey. But this route is long and should take more than a month if we can keep a good pace and we can give our feet a rest."

"That would be good. Later we can ride the rivers. There must be merchants using the waterways who would give us passage. One who would be kind to us without asking for fare," added Gilbert.

"I was thinking alike. It is far, and we will be hungry when we do not find food when ours is gone, but I suggest we do not tarry more than overnight in any place. This stop helped us recuperate from the cold winter trek, but while the skies are clearer and it warms we should go forth as long as it is light each day."

"Henricus. That is a good plan. I do not mind sleeping in the open, in a secluded spot where there is just the two of us. It has been a long time since we were alone."

He looked at her longingly, nodding and giving her hand a squeeze. "Tonight. I will find a place once we leave the lake area and head westward."

They traveled all morning and watched the sunrise over the snow-tipped mountains to the east. By midday they were on a road west of the lake after a steep incline around a mountain.

"Time to stop and eat," said Gilbert. "I have gotten out of practice during our time there, and my legs ache."

"Mine too. But it should be less of an upward climb once we clear this area. Just a little farther is the downward slope. I suggest we go a little farther, then we can stop in the lower levels where there is fresh water melting from the snows."

On the down slope they found a stream with cold water and a tree-lined bank. The water made a soothing sound as it rushed past, slowly wending its way to the streams and lakes below. The two tied the ass to a tree and unloaded a bit of their provisions.

Chapter Fifteen

Gilbert sat on a log at the edge of the cold water with her feet and toes wiggling in the stream. She looked up at the blue sky as Henricus came toward her and handed her some wine, a piece of bread, and some dried meat.

Gilbert ate slowly in silence. Henricus stared at her lovingly as she took her hood down and washed her face with the cool water. They finished their meal and he turned to her. Slowly he removed the rest of her clothing. It had been a long time since they were together, and before they continued, they coupled, glad to be alone.

They fell asleep in each other's arms, to wake in late afternoon, aware that they would have to move on and walk part of the evening in order to cover more ground that day. Luckily, the days were light longer and walking another few hours was not a problem. Dusk fell as they made their way farther west, content to be in nature again without the cold whipping around them and the struggle to keep warm.

chapter sixteen

The distance from Tegern to Lucerne was far. It took them some time to travel the over four hundred kilometers to finally see just before nightfall the reflection of the moon in the lake. Lake Lucerne has a complicated shape. Its arms bend and turn reaching out to the surrounding mountains. The runoff of the mountains formed a large lake with a changing irregular bank as melting snow poured down to the shore.

"Look at that," said Henricus.

"Beautiful. The moon is reflecting on the lake and it is like a mirror," she smiled. "The name Lucerne means oil lamp. You can imagine how that came to be."

"Come. This is a well-populated area. We should be able to find food and shelter, but be wary. There are twists and turns around the lake and with the reflection it is difficult to see where your footfall should be. We do not want to have injuries when we are making good progress now."

Gilbert added, "There is an old monastery here consecrated to St. Leodegar. I believe it is now dependent on the abbey of Murbach. We should go there. They are sure to take us in for a day, but let us not stay here too long. I want to keep moving. Just long enough to get some provisions and refresh ourselves."

"Yes. The next part is just a few days away. Five or six at most to Aventicum where we should be able to get someone to accommodate us to travel farther south by water," Henricus added.

Chapter Sixteen

Carefully they traversed around the lake marveling at the peaks of limestone and forests that stretched from the mountains to the shore. As they moved on they saw deer, a fox, chamois, and a marmot crossing their path.

"There it is," said Henricus as he spied the almost hundred-year-old monastery on the north side of the lake.

As they entered the abbey, the monks were all at dinner. They waited until the meal was finished and as the monks exited in silence, asked one quietly where they might find shelter and food for the night.

The monk nodded and led them to the kitchen and spoke to the cook.

"I will return after you have eaten." He did not tell them his name or welcome them, and seemed preoccupied with his own thoughts.

They were motioned to sit at a small wooden table in the kitchen where they were served the remnants of the meal that the monks had already consumed. Gilbert nodded at Henricus and motioned for them not to speak and just eat in silence. This abbey strictly observed the vow of silence during and after dinner and visitors had to comply. The monk returned after a while and motioned for them to follow as he escorted them to an empty cell containing two pallets of straw, a candle, and another wooden table smaller than the one they had just eaten from.

"We intend to leave tomorrow," Henricus said quietly. "Some food for our journey south would be very much appreciated if you can spare it."

The monk nodded and said quietly, "After morning prayers, go to the kitchen and they will provide what you need." He turned and walked out of the cell without another word.

Glad to be off their feet, Henricus whispered, "Let us rest now until morning prayers. We should sleep well after today's trek. But I think we should leave early tomorrow, before we arouse any interest in us and our journey."

"That is true. We do not want to call any attention to ourselves. It is not wise. Also, other than some food we really do not need to stay here. This is a large abbey and I do not want to be asked too many questions for fear that they may wonder at our travels. Some things need to be left unsaid. I have a goal in mind, and I do not want to be deterred having to stay somewhere longer than necessary."

Henricus hugged her and lay down exhausted from the day's travels.

"Good night my love," Gilbert whispered in his ear, then turned and went to her pallet, falling asleep immediately.

Gilbert's sleep was fitful. She dreamed and tossed about. Her inner thoughts bubbled to the surface, none of which were about the trip, but rather questions she had about different faiths and sects and how to reconcile each with the other. She longed to discuss these issues with Rabanus, but he was left far behind in Fulda. Sitting up after just a few hours, she looked out through the slit in the wall up to the dark sky. *Would there be someone like him when she finally got to Athens? Would there be learned men along the way to whom she might dialogue about the issues that pressed at her and weighed down her mind with wonder?* she thought.

Lying down on her mat, she again fell asleep, only soon to be wakened with the call to prayer. Henricus, having slept through the night, looked at her and said, "Why do you still look tired? We have long to travel today. Are you refreshed enough?"

"Enough," Gilbert replied a little too tersely, "I want to go on now and cannot tolerate delays."

Henricus was hurt. He looked upon their time together as an

Chapter Sixteen

adventure and the leadership he provided for their route and their provisions was the only way he knew how to make himself feel that he was protecting this self-sufficient companion.

Gilbert was preoccupied in her own thoughts and left the cell before him, oblivious to his reaction. She made her way to prayers and did not notice Henricus sat apart from her. She prayed and shuffled her feet. The monk next to her looked her way and motioned for her to stop fidgeting.

Henricus left immediately after prayers and went to the cellar to obtain the provisions that were prepared for their journey. When he got to the stable, Gilbert already was standing with the ass and ready to go.

"Come, hurry," she said to him.

As they left the abbey and walked through the adjoining field, Henricus worked up the courage to ask her, "Gilbert, are you angry with me? Did I do something to displease you?"

Lost in her own thoughts of theological questions she wanted answered, she looked up at him surprised. "Why do you say that? No, I am not angry at all, just anxious to be moving on."

"You were quite short with me this morning. I cannot read your thoughts. I am not a mind reader." His voice trembled as he spoke because he so loved her and did not want to argue.

Gilbert looked at him in surprise. "No, Henricus. I am not angry with you. I just need to talk to someone about the questions I have of faith. You know I cannot do that with you. Not that I do not love you less for that, but I must be frank with you. I cannot live without that dialogue. It is my life. You are my love."

Henricus was somewhat relieved, and realized at that moment that Gilbert would not always be his. He could not compete with her mind, which raced through material and made connections where none were apparent to him. She needed someone to provide guidance in that which he was not capable of even understanding. She was pulling away from him. As long as they were traveling, he was hers. They talked about the view, about their health traveling so far, about the length they had to travel to complete the day's voyage, but never about matters of theology. He cherished their talk of love and the exploration of each other's bodies, but the banality of delaying her in her mission was not in the preview of this humble, kind man.

It took six more days to get to Aventicum on Lake Murten after stopping each evening. Henricus made a point of engaging Gilbert in small talk, but her nature was to be introspective. She lived in her head, while he was more of the world. Knowing he would not raise above his present level, a scribe and illuminator wherever they went, he had to be content with the time he could spend with her.

For the next part of the journey they finally would be able to move by means other than their own two feet. Arriving at the water's edge they walked along until they found one of the powerful merchants on his way to Marseilles in a vessel. Goods and slaves were transported by river, all the way from these inland lakes to the river Rhodanus and then south to the Mediterranean Sea. The merchants traveled freely with the protection of the emperor who was in debt to them.

"Sir," Henricus asked a man who had a long beard with curls on either side hanging down under his hat. "We are weary monks, travelers who are making our way to Toulon. Would it be possible to travel with you and your goods downstream? We intend to sell our ass and can give you whatever profit we earn as passage."

The man looked up at the two ragged monks who sought passage with him. "I have little room, yet I will make space. Bring your own provisions and hurry. My other passengers are arriving and I am almost done loading my cargo."

Chapter Sixteen

Slaves and provisions were being stowed below deck as the two travelers turned to leave. While they were talking, another man walked up to the vessel, and the merchant greeted him with, "Come aboard, rabbi."

"Thank you, sir," said Henricus. "We will be back shortly."

As they walked away, Gilbert excitedly said, "He is a Jewish merchant, Henricus. The other is a rabbi, a learned man. Perhaps I can talk to him on the trip about matters for which I have questions."

"Yes. That will lift your spirits and provide much to talk about. But first, let us sell the ass and get back before they leave us at the river's edge."

In the small village, they found someone to buy the ass. Not knowing what the animal was worth, Henricus took the first offer and used some of the funds to purchase bread and wine for their journey. They hurried back to the boat, they boarded, gave the merchant the remainder of the money, and found a plank to sit on as a crew member pushed off into the river. The rabbi was deep in prayer sitting at the other end of the vessel.

Henricus told Gilbert to wait and not interrupt while the rabbi was deep in prayer. They would be on the boat for days and there would be plenty of time to speak to him.

Gilbert nodded, though she was so excited that she could do nothing except think about the questions she had for the man and deciding which to pose first.

Finally, weary from the trip, Gilbert lay down on the plank and fell asleep.

chapter eighteen

The vessel, on its way to Marseilles, procured its cargo of slaves and transported them for sale. Using gold purchased decrees from the emperor, they were under his protection in dealing with the cargo. By lending large sums to the realm that paid interest on the loans, the merchants engendered privileges. Proselytizing to the population, Christian or pagan, was one of the opportunities they were granted.

The old rabbi, Isahar, watched the two monks and saw this as another chance to try to educate Christians about his religion. They would be on the boat together for some time, and he was eager to spend the journey productively so was ready for Gilbert when she awoke and made her way over to where he sat.

As she stood, Henricus said, "Should I go with you? You must be wary of his spell. He will try to convince you to change to his faith. I was told that in Mainz. They persist until all argument against is to no avail."

"Do not worry. I think I will be able to resist. After all, working with Rabanus prepared me well to debate matters of theology. Will you join us?"

"No. I am going to talk to the captain. This procedure for commerce in flesh is of interest to me. I know the tradition of slavery is ancient, but the sanction for those who themselves were enslaved is incongruous."

Chapter Eighteen

Gilbert nodded saying, "Be careful not to criticize. This is their livelihood. If you do, they may put us off the vessel."

Henricus nodded and frowned thinking, *She does not think I have the tact to do that?*

She made her way next to the rabbi. Henricus walked away thinking to himself that this was their fate when they got to Athens. She would go her way and he another. Although not to his liking, he was resigned and increasingly less sure of his future with her.

He found the merchant standing near the railing barking orders to the men. He was angry at them for not making better progress. "Time is fleeting and you are costing me money. Move faster, all of you. We have a schedule and a deadline to get these slaves to market for the auction."

Henricus tried to make conversation with the man, still gruff from yelling.

"What do you want?"

"Nothing, sir. I thought perhaps you might enlighten me as to this commerce. I have heard of the transport of slaves, yet have never encountered such."

"What do you want to know? Are you thinking of starting this business yourself?" he answered snidely.

"No, of course not. I understand that only your kind may engage in such transport in France."

"Yes. I have my papers. Are you sent here to check that I am so credentialed?"

"No. I am but a poor monk traveling from an abbey in Germany to Athens to study. We both are. We have traveled far, and I am just anxious for conversation. My companion does not speak much and is more interested in talking to the rabbi. So I thought I might speak to you. But if you are too busy, I understand."

The merchant, softening and taking pity on this mere boy, told him to come to his cabin and he would answer any questions he had. "Follow me and I will explain."

Careful to walk and speak as a man would, Gilbert introduced herself to Isahar and asked if she might sit near him to pass the time. The old man looked up and thought, *If I can convince this boy, the captain will give back my fare for the journey.* "Certainly," he said nodding to a seat on a box close to where he sat.

"I want to introduce myself. I am Gilbert and am a humble monk traveling to Athens to study. My fellow traveler is Henricus."

"And where come you from?"

"From Fulda. We were there for some time working at the abbey."

"Ah, you are literate then, I presume, since their library and scribes are known. What was your work there? And your companion?"

"Henricus worked in the cellar and is a fine illuminator. I scribed and worked with Rabanus, the abbot."

"You are young to have worked with him. Are you not? What special gifts you must possess to have been in his confidence." Isahar knew that this was a smart one if she had been engaged with Rabanus.

Gilbert was taken aback. This man knew of Rabanus and of the special requirements to work with him. "Yes, I was fortunate to be of aid to him," she said as humbly as possible.

"Do not be modest. You must read Latin and Greek. Am I not correct?"

She nodded.

"Ah, and you are going to Athens to study further, I presume."

"Yes." Gilbert was reluctant to say anything further, wanting to concentrate on what this man could give her as insight into his

Chapter Eighteen

perspectives of religion. Yet, there was something about him that alerted her to be suspicious of his quick insight and knowledge. She would proceed cautiously and discuss only matters of faith.

"Would you care to spend our time on this vessel talking about the Talmud? It may add to your learning by hearing another point of view." He smiled and with a twinkle in his eye said, "Perhaps I may even sway you to understand my faith and be sympathetic to our rituals." He thought being open with her would engender sympathy for his purpose.

Gilbert, hungry to proceed, said, "Yes. Please go on. I understand your teachings are a dialogic. May I ask questions and thus provide a give and take to your arguments?"

"Of course. That is what we do in the yeshiva. It is a logical deductive process, much like Socratic dialogue, which I presume you are familiar with and have read about."

"Yes. Of course. Where would you like to begin?" She was eager to get on with it.

"Let us start with the myths that have been recognized as perpetuating and suppressing the truth. I do not use the word truth lightly. I believe that there is one Lord. All that has followed is a corruption of the truth. Let me elaborate."

Gilbert sat quietly intent on listening to his narrative, citing scripture, verse and line, to corroborate what he believed was the truth. She did not argue that his narrative was scurrilous. Instead she waited patiently as he described a Jesus as purveyor of a kind of magical sorcery, urged on by John, thereby amassing followers with stories of apparent miracles. Item by item, he provided explanations and elaborations on the last supper, death, resurrection, and the veneration of Jesus as the son of the Lord. And when he exhausted hours of narrative, he called for tea and rested.

Not having participated at all, Gilbert sat in silence as she pondered the politics of religion, and how the narratives and stories grew as followers reinterpreted the stories for their own use. This Jew, a member of a persecuted faith, believed that the source of Christianity was a myth. Not that Jesus did not live, but did so as a man on earth.

Henricus came over to her and asked how the interaction with the rabbi was.

"I do not know. So far I have just listened, not sure if he is telling me what he believes or what he wants me to hear. I think he is intent on trying to convert me. I assume we are going to resume after tea, and, if you want, sit in. I am going to engage him next time."

"You need me to support you in arguing with him? I doubt that!" he said sarcastically.

"No, but you should hear what he has to say. You know Henricus that you are more religious and pious than I. My interest is in the learning, in knowing the world and what has been written of it. In invention and exploration. There is so much to know. So much to be discovered. I view the bible as a narrative that has been used for good and ill. For control and for profit. It was written by people who believed. Learned people. But I cannot just blindly believe without doubt. This is just one more version that he presents. But come sit. Isahar returns."

Isahar sat down and looked at Henricus. "We are now three. Shall I go back and reiterate?"

"No. I can narrate the previous for Henricus later. I would like to ask you some questions. Is that all right?"

Isahar nodded, stroking his beard. "What would you like to ask?"

"If you reject Jesus as savior, what then is your people's

Chapter Eighteen

conception of God?" Gilbert said seriously. "How do you reconcile the following of Jesus's words by so many, many more than follow yours, if it is libelous in your opinion?"

"I do not have to reconcile anything. We are more ancient than your belief, much older in trying to bring the truth to the world, to provide an ethos of living, one that is inclusive and much less damaging and aggressive. Truth is often persecuted, and surely you know the history of my people. My God is one that watches all; that brought you the Ten Commandments and tenets of living. One of community and family, one that is spiritual and mystical, still it does recognize others who do not believe. We want to live and prosper and have been reduced to stereotypes forced to wander after expulsion from lands where we were long before Jesus, a Jew, was born. My God is benevolent, one who gave us heaven and earth and prescribed a way of life that is in concert with the earth. We do not kill those who do not think the way we do, do not force others to renounce their religion and take on ours. We want to be left alone, while we have been reduced and characterized as misers and heretics. We make deals with emperors just to live and do their dirty work because there is no other way. Our God is everywhere, sees all, knows all, and watches over our struggles to survive."

Isahar was getting worked up now, uncharacteristically for him. But his audience was so young, the ages of his grandchildren, and he wanted them to know the theology they held by inheritance was not the only way.

"Rabbi, please calm yourself. Yes, we are young, but we are thinking people, and the evidence you have presented is contrary to what we have been taught and believe. There is comfort in our beliefs, just as I presume there is in yours. It provides a way of life, just as does yours. But it provides a great deal of hope also in that there is a mortality that, if you follow, leads to everlasting peace after death. That is comforting. That is something real we can bring to those who try to cheat and steal, kill and maim. It can deter them from a way of life that is not in the teachings of Jesus."

"Yet, it is in the name of Jesus that your people proselytize and force others to follow, who actively coerce the acceptance of an alien sect from their own, and banish and kill those who do not. Someday the emperor will lose interest in us as their merchants, and we will have to flee. Someday someone will expel us once again just for our beliefs. Someday they will try to wipe us off the face of the earth. Is that benevolent, is that kind, is that moral?"

Henricus and Gilbert sat and listened. She had no response to this and just sat deep in thought saying only, "What terrible things people do in the name of religion."

"Children, I am tired. I have to rest. Nightfall is here and I have a trying day once we dock at Lugdunum. Please excuse me." He rose and went belowdecks to lie down.

Henricus and Gilbert silently went to their pallets and closed their eyes, she deep in thoughts she did not share with him.

Chapter Nineteen

The boat docked in Lugdunum in calm weather and Henricus and Gilbert thanked the captain and said their good-byes to Isahar. Anxious and rested, yet hungry, they made their way to shore and were directed to the abbey where, Gilbert thought, *they could perhaps kiss the hand of the only living saint, Agobardo.* The archbishop of Lugdunum was old and set in his beliefs, which were famous for two things. The first was the promotion of the unity of church and state. He had spent most of his time in power embroiled in the politics of France trying to cement the unity he promoted vigorously. He was a powerful influence but was not able to convince the emperor to share power with the Church. The second was his notorious attacks on the Jewish population.

Operating under the protections imparted by the son of Charlemagne, Louis the Pious, the swath of Jewish privileges included a prohibition on Christians proselytizing to them. Jews engendered legal protections of trade and commerce and were not forced to baptize slaves. Agobardo wrote tracts on anti-Judaism and campaigned against what he saw as a dangerous growth of power and influence of Jewish merchants that was contrary to the law of a church intent on converting everyone. His was a vendetta aimed to stop the heretics and end their culture, thereby creating a Catholic France as influential as the realm.

The two travelers entered the abbey with Rabanus's introduction in hand, hoping to ask for help in the continuation of their travels. Dirty and hungry, they were ushered humbly into Agobardo's presence and bowed in front of him to kiss his ring. Agobardo held out his hand as each in turn paid homage to the saint.

Gilbert handed him the letter of introduction from Rabanus and, as a result, was warmly greeted.

Recognizing their state of need, Agobardo bade them, "Rise before you faint. You look like you need to rest here and take nourishment." He scanned their dirty ragged clothes and worn footwear. "What brings you two to this humble abbey?" the old man spoke haltingly.

"We do need rest. We have traveled far, mostly by foot from Fulda, then by vessel to Lugdunum. We are now on our way to Rhodanus to go by water to Arela. We would be grateful for any provisions you can offer, and a good night's rest before we are on our way," Henricus said.

"Surely we can accommodate you. I would like to invite you to share my frugal dinner table, but first my assistant will show you to a place you can rest and restore yourselves." He motioned for them to follow the monk who took them to a cell where they rested until evening.

A monk came to show them the way to prayers and then to dinner where each was seated alongside Agobardo. Unlike the abbeys in Mainz and Fulda where meals were taken in silence, he talked to the two, making quiet conversation throughout the meal.

"What kind of vessel transported you here?" he asked.

"A merchant, a Jew, whose vessel was transporting slaves. We sold our ass and paid him for transport. There was a rabbi on board and it made for good conversation to pass the time. From

Chapter Nineteen

here it is all by boat. Perhaps we can find some chores on the vessel to pay for our passage," Henricus answered.

"Ah, yes. They are a problem, those children of the devil. They try to convert you. There is no end to their lies, and they have the protection of the emperor. I have tried to convince him otherwise. I have written much on this scourge. They are protected by the realm, but my work is to unite the Church and the emperor's people so that hopefully those Jews will lose their privileges and be either converted or exiled."

Gilbert looked at him in wonder. *Should I speak and refute his logic? Should I remain silent and listen to this patter? I think this angers me, but this must remain hidden. He is a saint, he is powerful, and he has won many battles within the Church and with the realm, and nothing I can say will change his mind.* She looked at Henricus who looked worried that she would open her mouth and talk back to the abbot, so she put up her hand and motioned for him not to worry about her.

After the meal, Agobardo gave them both his blessing, advice on how to proceed to their next destination, and said he would provide introduction for them to the nunnery in Arela where they could replenish themselves.

They returned to their cell and found a new pair of shoes for each lying on the floor, clean robes, and money to pay for the next part of their journey.

"This is a surprise," said Henricus.

"Yes, he is full of contradictions. Pious and giving, yet he has a vendetta against the Jews that is not rational at all and does nothing but promulgate a stereotype that is powerful and potentially very detrimental to them. He is old and perhaps this too will pass with him."

"I think not, Gilbert. He is well published, and his tracts are disseminated throughout the Church. I fear his views will grow and expand rather than diminish."

"I hope not. Knowledge and questioning is to be encouraged, not stifled. To irrationally damn a whole belief system without cause can be used for evil when in the hands of people who have much to gain from such," she said pensively. "There is so much contradiction in dogma. While inclusive, it is restrictive; while caring and spiritual, it is cruel and disparaging of those who are not congruent in their beliefs."

"There is nothing to do about this here. The emperor has accepted the Jews and they are under his protection. Agrogardo has not convinced him otherwise. That is enough for now. There are other places for the Jews to garner the same protections," Henricus yawned, tired from the day and the travel and the discussion.

"Yes, but someone has to lead the Church so as to promulgate different views of acceptance. Too many have been persecuted and have died in the name of religion," she added getting more worked up at the injustice.

"I am retiring. You should too. We have to get to Rhodanus tomorrow and obtain passage to Arelas."

Henricus closed his eyes and fell asleep immediately. Gilbert stayed awake for a while re-creating the conversations with Agobardo and Isahar. Finally, she wore herself out thinking and slept too.

It took six days to get to Arelas. They paid for passage and obtained provisions with the funds provided by the abbot. Debarking at the dock, they sought an abbey and were told there was a nearby nunnery established by St. Caesarious in the sixth century.

As they approached the gate, they came upon a watchman sleeping in the midday sun. The two walked by him and entered a

Chapter Nineteen

courtyard with not a person in sight. All was quiet so they walked around until they wandered into the dormitory where all the inhabitants were sleeping. Wearing not their habits but nightdresses, Henricus, who had never seen any women undressed except for Gilbert, could not avert his eyes from the array of bodies in their see-through outerwear. Some of the nuns were from Arabia, others were Swiss, still others of all shades and sizes, their bosoms rising and falling with their breath. Just then an Arabic clock rang and the sleeping nuns began to wake.

Frozen in place, the nuns rose and circled the two male visitors, never before seen in their private quarters. The light from the windows further defined their fine figures, and Henricus had to look away to calm himself.

"We are sorry to have disturbed you, but no one was in the courtyard to speak to and by accident we wandered into your bedchamber," Gilbert finally said, tugging at Henricus's sleeve to pull him out into the common area so the nuns could cover modestly and put their habits back on.

She looked at Henricus once they were in the open and could see the flush on his cheeks. "You need to calm yourself and stay in character here. This is not the same as staying in an abbey. We are young boys in a sea of women here, and whether they truly are chaste or not, and they probably are not, this is only a short sojourn for us and then we have to be going. We do not want to be undone by these women, nor do we want to abuse the privilege of staying here for a few days."

A young nun came over, bade them follow to the tables in the dining area, and offered them food that they had never before eaten. Figs, raisins, and other sweet delights, as well as the greens and vegetables of southern France, were laid before them. They ate heartily, enjoying the delicacies too much for humble monks, and decided to spend a few days in the nunnery before heading to Toulon for the long sail on the Mediterranean.

By the third day, they were well fed and satisfied when Gilbert took sick. She stopped eating, had stomach troubles, and spoke in three languages words that Henricus could not discern. She stood, she sat, she wandered, and she took to bed. He, who had spent three days in the company of other women, who had never before been treated with such kindness and openness of character after their travels mired in deception and depravation, was joyous. But Gilbert, who was less ill of body than of mind, was experiencing something she had never before. Jealousy.

"What is the matter Gilbert? Can I get you anything?" he asked.

She cried in their chamber, and she reproached him for spending too much time with the others. He tried to hold her and kiss her. She rebuffed him, telling him to go and kiss one of the other nuns.

After weeks and weeks to no avail, the nuns told Henricus to take Gilbert to a cave near the waterfall below that was the site of a miracle. He packed provisions and set out with her and, when they were halfway there, Gilbert seemed to be coming back to herself. By the time they found the cave and he lit a fire for the night, Gilbert was clear eyed and looking at him in a way he had not seen for a long time. She sat demurely at his feet and leaned back toward him. Lifting her hand slowly toward his, she sobbed and said, "I am a fool, Henricus. I had no idea that love could drive you into such a rage that you get sick. Can you forgive me? You have been so patient, so good to me."

He stroked her hair and turned her face toward his, and she saw he too was crying.

Gilbert stood up and removed her clothes. He did the same, and, placing their robes on the ground, they slowly made love.

Chapter Nineteen

Never returning to the nunnery, they stayed in the cave for a few days before making their way toward Toulon. They had stayed in Arela a total of three months; Gilbert was sick with jealousy for most of the time. They both learned a lesson from this experience. First, that she was committed to him and him to her, and that they really loved each other. Second, life placed obstacles and trials in the path of true love, and they needed to be vigilant to sustain it.

Chapter Twenty

The port was empty as they neared, except for one Venetian galley. The boat's charter was to carry the remains of Mark the Evangelist to a basilica to be dedicated to the saint in Venice. The two Venetian merchants, with the help of Greek monks, stowed the relic on the boat under a layer of pork so that the Muslims would not touch the covering. From Venice, the vessel went to Provence to purchase slaves to be exchanged in faraway ports of the Orient for herbs, cotton, and other relics. That is where Henricus and Gilbert encountered the boat and the cargo of slaves being led aboard.

They waited at the dock for the Jewish merchant to finish his dealings with the owner who was making final arrangements for the cargo that would board the vessel.

"Is there no morality here?" Gilbert pondered out loud as she eyed the shipment of human beings.

Henricus shrugged. "It keeps the conquered from being slaughtered so I guess that is a sort of morality. It has always been so. The only thing that changes is the people who are conquered. That is history and we cannot interfere."

"Those who are slaves become those who enslave. I understand, but in many cases it is being done in the name of God. The Church is culpable here and condones these acts as it enriches its coffers as a result," Gilbert said worriedly. "If I were in charge, I would try to find a way to stop this cycle. Trafficking in the flesh is wrong."

Chapter Twenty

"What would happen if there were no slaves? Isn't the possibility worse than the reality? Who would be the building workers, the farmers, and the toilers? How would commerce be conducted? You know the route. These slaves are just one part of a trade that brings necessities and desires to the population everywhere. Before you condemn, think about the consequences. We also need these people to help us so do not say a word within their hearing to undermine their endeavor with morality talk," Henricus added.

"What about a fair and equitable wage, then, for those who toil; one that does not enslave people to tasks, but rewards them for their work? There must be an alternative," Gilbert said.

They were interrupted by the owner who passed on his way to the ship; whip in one hand and a tether in the other, he was followed by sixteen slaves, mostly men, but some women and two young boys. He led them on board, handing the rope to one of his crew who walked them down to the lower depths of the vessel. He turned his head in the direction of our two travelers, noting their emaciated state, and thought, *These two look like they want to get on board. I can transport them along with this catch and put them to work keeping order during the trip. They can help keep the calm and avoid trouble from the slaves on the voyage. Only executioners and priests have that effect on those in bondage,* he thought as he approached Gilbert and Henricus.

"You are waiting here for a vessel?" he asked.

"Yes," Henricus said before Gilbert could speak her mind. "We are bound for Athens, yet any vessel taking us close to those shores would be welcome. We have a small amount of money to pay, very little, but we can lend a hand to pay for our trip."

"I could use you both. You are welcome to come aboard the *Saint Buchard*. I am headed for Alexandria, but can get you close to your goal if you want. The route is circuitous for purposes of trade with the first stop being Corsica in three days. Eventually we will get close to Athens on our way to our final destination."

"That would be fine. Thank you, sir," Gilbert said.

The two rose on unsteady, weary legs and boarded, seating themselves on a pile of ropes. Soon the ship pulled away from the dock. The oars dipped into the sea as the sun, as calm as glass, warmed them on the last part of their journey. Gilbert and Henricus, closer than ever after the episode at the nunnery, leaned on each other for comfort.

Their service as those who bring calm to the slaves was not needed, so they spent the next three days lolling in the sun. Sleeping on and off, replenishing their energy with food and drink, the two were relaxed and serene as they admired the scenery, the sunrise, and the sunsets along the way.

On the third day, they landed on the eastern shores of Corsica in the French community of Aleria. Here the vessel would take on fresh water and replenish stores. With hours on their own, the two travelers disembarked as the captain remarked, "Make sure you are well back before we leave port. We wait for no one. Remember, before sunrise and we are off."

"We will, sir," replied Henricus.

"Come, Henricus. We can see some of the famous relics residing on this island. We have the day and can see the important ones before coming back to board the ship. They will sail at dawn."

"Yes. I am anxious to get off this vessel for a while," said Henricus, stretching his legs.

They both knew that there were many relics on the island, and after asking for directions, they went in search of them. They first headed to see the most famous relic, the rod of Moses, the staff with which he parted the sea, produced water from a rock, and

Chapter Twenty

was transformed into a snake and back. From this, they sought out the clod of earth that Adam was created from, and the rib of the Apostle Barnabas. There was also a vial containing milk from the Virgin Mary, a piece of woven cloth attributed to her, and some other relics that made their way via trade throughout the known world.

On their way back to the vessel before sailing, Gilbert said, "Henricus, it is curious that these objects are known to be authentic, or are they authentic only in their value for trade?"

"What do you mean? They are sacred and have been authenticated by authorities. Places of worship have been built to house them and are named for the relics they possess."

"Yes, but how are they known to be real, some saved for over 800 years, others much older. Is this the rod, or is this the cloth? Surety is only in the authentication by word of mouth, yet look at the pilgrims who come to see them, who kneel at their cases and pray on their knees to what may only be a piece of cloth."

"Are you denying the power of the relic to engender awe and piousness?"

"No, Henricus. I am merely observing the strength of belief in these people who accept on faith that these objects are what others say they are. Most people question nothing, and their short lives are filled with passivity and acceptance."

"Are you saying the Church causes this passivity?" Henricus asked.

"No, but acceptance often means to be passive in accepting the Church's doctrine without question. I am asking if that is a good thing or an evil to keep people ignorant of inquiry and dialogue."

She was working herself up to a full argument and starting to quote scripture and verse when they approached the ship at the ready to pull up anchor and sail toward Sardinia. That seemed to still her as Henricus, tired of the dialogue, went to watch the crew prepare for departure.

With first light and a strong wind, they flew past Sardinia and spent days in rougher seas, seasick and vomiting from the rolling waves until they became accustomed to the motion. The slaves too were not faring well, and Henricus and Gilbert, when they themselves were not too green from the motion of the boat, had to calm them down and remind them that they would be saved and alive when they reached their destination.

The routine and laziness of the days passed without event. After two months on board they disembarked at Corinth, forty-eight miles west of Athens.

"This is as close as I can get you," said the captain, "but to thank you for helping along the way, I am entrusting a Greek slave to lead you to Athens. This is Theonas. He will ensure you successfully complete your journey through Megara and deliver you to your destination in Athens where you can turn him over to the Church as a worker in my name."

Henricus nodded, "Thank you, captain. We will follow your orders and hope the rest of your voyage is successful."

The captain laughed, "It will be certainly when we sell these slaves and pick up our next cargo to return to the route we just came from. It is a very lucrative business I am in, as long as we deliver the goods in a timely manner."

Gilbert started to protest, but Henricus took her arm and led her off the ship so as not to anger the man who had brought them safely so close to their final destination. She scowled and bit her lip, and off they went following Theonas in silence.

When he was ahead of them out of hearing distance, Henricus said, "Do not even suggest what you are thinking, Gilbert."

Chapter Twenty

"And what do you think I am imagining, Henricus," she said snippily.

"You want to free him when we get there, don't you?"

She looked away, unable to gaze at his face.

"Well, you cannot interfere in this. We are not to change the order of things, not when we have benefited from the commerce. Let it be. We are soon to reach our goal and some day you may be in a position to speak out, but not now."

Henricus walked on ahead of her out of earshot before she could answer.

Chapter Twenty-One

The travelers at last entered Athens on a cloudless, sun-filled day. Crowds of people streamed into churches to celebrate the Sunday of Orthodoxy, commemorating the restoration of the holy images. The strict ruler, Theophilus, had outlawed image worshipping and punished not only those who worshipped them but also those who created the holy relics, the monks. Upon his death, Theodora II, his wife, an ardent image worshipper, reinstated the practice by convening a synod in Constantinople to restore them throughout the Byzantine realm. For this celebration day, followers came to kiss the icons returned to them so recently.

Some women glued their children's hair on images of the Virgin, monks made offerings of their shaved hair, and women scraped paint off the icons and mixed it with water, downing the concoction as did some priests who mixed it with wine from the sacrifice. Ultimately, the bishop had to cover the icons in glass so that they could survive the fervency of the people and further destruction by ardent followers.

The three followed the crowd and entered the temple of Theseus, which was transformed into a Christian church dedicated to St. George. Hardly a place was found for them to stand so crowded was the church. They found a small space in a narrow corner of the sanctuary. The bishop of Athens, Niketas, stood up front wearing

Chapter Twenty-One

embroidered robes the likes of which the two humble monks had never seen before. Gold threads adorned his cloak and a golden hat rose on his pate. Their prior experience was the preacher of poverty to the faithful with the promise of riches in Paradise, not in the material world, and all this was new to them.

"Henricus, look at his robes. Is this the way in the Church of Athens, and are we humble monks the ones who are out of step? It seems incongruous to me. What purpose does it serve to preach in finery to those in need dressed in garb that the followers can never aspire to?" Gilbert whispered to her companion.

"Perhaps we are just used to the Benedictine way we have learned, and this is the norm everywhere else?" Henricus answered, not knowing what else to say in reply.

Niketas began an interminably long service that, in fact, was a shortened version yet was quietly listened to by the followers. Those standing near the three stared at their dress and manner, their short shaved hair, bald pate, and coarse clothing. At the end of the service, after receiving the communion bread, the three were encircled by a throng of people who began to ask questions regarding their situation.

"Are you not ashamed to cut your beard?" one asked.

"What manner of clothing do you wear?" another posed.

"We are Benedictine monks from Germany. This is our habit in our country, and we follow the tradition of our order there. We are committed to poverty, penance, and sacrifice," Gilbert answered in flawless Greek.

Henricus just stood there impatiently for a time, then tried to create a path so they could exit the church. Before they could move, the bishop, who also noticed the three, came to them and set them free of their inquisitors, scolding the followers for troubling the newcomers.

"Follow me," he nodded and the flock parted as he walked to his litter.

The two monks were told by his aide to follow the bishop onto his litter and seat themselves on the opposite side facing him. Eight men served as bearers and conveyed them to the palace at the foot of the Acropolis. He alighted, and the two followed the bishop while their slave walked behind the litter. They found themselves in a large shaded area under an arbor where there was laid out a sumptuous banquet in celebration of the icon restorations.

The bishop motioned for one of the servants to lead their faithful guide away, and Gilbert said to him, "He is a gift to you from the captain who transported us on the sea hoping for a kind word in his behalf from the bishop."

"I will say a prayer for him and a blessing for delivering you safely to our shores." Niketas smiled.

"Look," Henricus said. "The trees bend under the weight of the jars and vessels hanging from them."

"Yes. There are many seats," she noted, "and I believe the other guests are arriving. This should prove interesting. They are a group looking no better off than we are, some worse."

The monks, hermits, and ascetics appearing had become exiled during the reign of Theophilus, living in the open with animals to avoid forsaking the icons that were an integral part of their belief. Some had fasted, all were unclean, and sores shown on another, while most had not had cooked food for some time. Those who fled to the mountains came with canes supporting their frail frames, and all were welcomed by the bishop and shown to a seat as the meal was brought to the tables.

Gilbert and Henricus, while not clean themselves, were forced to hold their noses to quell the stench emanating from these men.

Chapter Twenty-One

The bishop himself appeared to not flinch at the odor, smiling and gracious to all.

The ambitious and courtly Niketas was compelled to make much of them, since these men, once restored, were part of his grand plan for restoring dominance of the Church now that the mixture of doctrine and iconography had been reconciled.

Joining this ragged group were two professors of Greek, an astrologer, and three eunuchs from the Byzantine court, who had brought to Athens the imperial edict for the restoration of the holy images and had been invited to the episcopal table.

When all had taken their places and the messianic psalms had been recited, Niketas cut a piece of bread and offered it on a silver plate to the image of the Virgin who always received the first portion. Turning to his guests, he declared, "Let us enjoy and savor our meal, the first of many as we restore order to the Church." Niketas knew he needed all their help, and this was the first part of his plan to engender support.

Cutting into a fat goat stuffed with onions, garlic, and leeks, this course was followed by fishes seasoned with caviar and mutton with honey and raisins. It was a sumptuous, aromatic meal.

Henricus and Gilbert, accustomed to bread and ale and occasionally meat, all unseasoned as was German food, took spoons in hand and tentatively tasted these Byzantine delicacies.

Henricus, cup in hand, tried the wine placed before him and whispered to Gilbert, "Oh, it tastes of resin. I cannot drink this."

"Nor I. But be careful not to offend. Luckily they do not understand our tongue," Gilbert cautioned as the monk beside her offered to refill her glass. She waved her hand to stop his pouring.

Wise Niketas noticed their plight and ordered some roast pigeons to be set before them, some honey from Hymettus, and pure Chian wine. Relieved, Gilbert nodded to the bishop seated across from them and held her cup out to honor him before taking a sip. He nodded at her, smiled, and lifted his glass to return the toast.

During the rest of the dinner, the old monks returned from exile told of the miracles they encountered while away, amazing tales of fantasy. One told of how he was taken in by a poor man who had nothing to share with him. The monk put a grain of wheat in the poor man's beard, and when he shook his head, it yielded sacks of wheat. Another planted his wand of office in the garden of a monastery by an abbot's grave and in three years there grew apples, peaches, cherries, figs, and grapes to feed all the brothers. The bishop only had interest in the two young novices and spent much of the time talking to them as the aesthetes droned on.

"You have traveled here from Germany for what purpose? Who sent you?"

"Rabanus suggested we come here. I was his assistant in his great work, the encyclopedia, helping him for some time. I am fluent in Greek and Latin, and after debating with him all matters of theology, he felt that I could further my education by coming to this great seat of learning," said Gilbert.

"We are both scribes. I am an illuminator, but Gilbert is seeking to broaden his education so we set out with this letter from Rabanus to your Holiness to see if we could remain here and continue our leaning and be of use to your flock," Henricus added in German with a sprinkling of Greek, but Gilbert was quick to fill in the gaps.

Niketas engaged the two monks and the Byzantine eunuchs in questions of dogma, and asked Gilbert about the Eucharist and whether those from his region believed that the bread and wine were changed into the body and blood of the savior, or whether they were a symbol.

Chapter Twenty-One

Gilbert, unsure of which of these positions the bishop ascribed to, began to skirt the issue with the implications of each position arguing for either, as appropriate. Finally, based on the parry, she figured out that the Byzantine world believed in true conversion, and so as not to offend him, she demurred. They went on to discuss the Virgin and other matters, and Gilbert asked him why those of the Eastern Church did not cut off their hair as St. Paul recommended. The bishop evaded the answer, and they parried on.

Night fell, and the two travelers, having finally reached their destination, were sated with food and especially drink so both yawned and asked to be excused. They wandered outside and walked among the marbled statues of the Acropolis, which was lit by the moonlight. Gilbert sat down on a marble bench and Henricus sat down at her feet, pointing to the temple of the Wingless Victory and hoping that their bliss would last forever. After kissing and lovemaking, the two fell asleep in each other's arms.

Chapter Twenty-Two

"Come, come, Henricus. Wake up. The city and Acropolis beckon, and I am anxious to take in all that they offer."

Gilbert's excitement was contagious, and Henricus, rubbing the sleep from his eyes, stood up and smiled at her.

"Your wish is my command, dear one," he said, adorningly mocking her with a bow.

Gilbert looked at him and was at a loss to understand the subtlety of what he said. Henricus was only half jesting yet thought, *She ignores me if I am serious or I am not. Nothing I do catches her attention she is so engrossed in herself.*

"To the summit of the Acropolis then. The center of all the activity here," she nodded, walking off ahead of him as he followed like a dog waiting for a morsel to be thrown to him from its master.

As they walked, a crowd of Athenians followed, curious at the newcomers and their clothes. The two Benedictines, intent on exploring the city, interacted with no one so intent were they to see the sights.

"Look at that. What was a statue now has erected upon its site a wooden cross. Small churches covered by vaults arise all over making them look like mere huts." Henricus noticed.

"Yes, but there are monks everywhere sitting at the entrances and ascetics scraping their sores or poring over ancient manuscripts

Chapter Twenty-Two

for the inscription of legends, some weaving baskets, breakfasting on onions, and perhaps thanking God that they had been born Greeks and not the barbarians that conquered them," she replied.

Henricus was looking at the women, but Gilbert took no notice until he said out loud, "My goodness, they are so beautiful here."

Gilbert looked around at the women and their children and the modesty of the maidens who wrapped their long robes around their bodies, veils over their faces and all the while clinging to their mothers' sides. *It is so different from the thickness of the German women. So foreign to my own upbringing, this obeisance and protection offered by the mothers. This is the way it should be,* she thought.

"They look only at the ground to avoid puddles and missteps, and they blush so especially when the wind catches their garments and disturbs their modesty," Henricus went on, clearly intrigued by the maidens.

"I believe that the Byzantines came here for the women of the emperor's harem," she said with not a tinge of jealousy that Henricus was admiring another.

She walked on and, having passed the Tower of the Winds, came upon the marketplace, the agora.

"It is so large," Gilbert said to Henricus, "over thirty acres with three stoa where there sit men teaching others. And there are theaters also. I see two at least that must perform the plays I read about, even Aristophanes, comedies and tragedies alike."

"There is a gymnasium, courthouse. There are some poor souls being led by chains around their neck toward that building there. That must be a prison."

"Temples, five of them, and the sculptures of the gods and goddesses adorn each," Gilbert marveled. "This is the center of education, politics, religion, oratory, philosophy, and art, all combined. This is where I must come and learn."

The two stood incredulous at all the activity of this forum, and they noticed bishops and magistrates alike buying their own leeks for their daily meal. As they reached the Painted Porch, the scene changed. Instead of philosophers, they found astrologers, seers, interpreters of dreams, diviners of the future, and professors who sold their honey to earn funds since their teaching needed supplementary income to sustain them.

"Gilbert, it is getting late. We should find the monastery of Daphnium. Those kind monks have offered us shelter." She nodded, and off they went in search of the site.

For the next ten days they visited the antiquities, churches, and surroundings of Athens, and in the evening, they returned to the hospitality of the monastery where they were offered permanent lodging.

By the tenth day, Gilbert said to Henricus, "We cannot stay here. Their diet is not to our liking, the prayers are endless, and this place is so dirty, straw on the beds, and not where I want to be. But mostly, they do not wash every day, if even once a week, and reek of odor. This place is too severe and not anything we have come to know in either Mainz or Fulda. I would rather sleep in the street than spend more time here."

"I agree. There must be something more tolerable."

Not far from the monastery, there was a hermitage, a cell deserted since the death of its inhabitant, the monk St. Hermylus. Finding it on one of their walks, Henricus went inside and, when he came out, said, "Here. This is where we will go. Let us take over this hut and make it our own."

"Yes," Gilbert agreed, "and with our meager monies, the first thing we will purchase is a thick mattress, then a spit, a copper kettle, olive oil, goats, fowl, and a dog for protection."

Gilbert, having been treated like a slave by her stepmother,

Chapter Twenty-Two

knew all about cooking and making a place habitable. In a corner, she hung the skull of the former occupant as a talisman for the future. She set about the task as she did everything else, in a systematic way. She learned to bargain at the market, barter with others, and, in exchange for lessons, earned money teaching at the agora alongside the others. Eventually she attracted admirers who came to her hut and paid to be taught by the learned, young, fair monk.

Gilbert woke early, milked the goats, boiled eggs, gathered cherries, and then woke Henricus.

"Breakfast is ready. You can clean up. I am off to the monks to get new books. Plato, I think, awaits me. They do not read them and I am the only borrower."

"I am awake." He stood and ate, put away the remnants of the meal, then went to catch fish and reset his rabbit snares. Later he tilled the soil in the garden and did other chores before she returned.

"What are you writing?" he asked.

"Some tracts that I intend to sell for extra money. They are selling well and I have actually had requests for others."

Each evening she spread a table in front of the door under an old tree and laid out a meal of the products of the garden, and whatever Henricus caught that day fishing or hunting. Their meal was unique on the mountain. The Greek monks were scandalized by the odors and strangeness of the Benedictine's diet and made the sign of the cross as they passed.

Henricus could not help smiling, often laughing out loud, at their reaction to their dinner fare. But eventually one or another stopped in to terrify the meat eaters into submission.

"How can you eat the flesh of animals?" one asked. "It is a sacrilege, and the flames of hell will consume you," the one yelled, but his taste buds belied his true feelings as saliva fell from the corners of his mouth. His companion agreed, though too could not stifle his own juices.

Gilbert offered the tastiest morsels to them both, holding out a spoon to each of fish in broth. "Try a little, and then if you cannot take it in I say that is all right. But do not begrudge us our fare."

These monks who ate no meat nor anything that flew or swam tasted a little and quickly passed the spoon back and forth to Gilbert for more. After that it was not unusual for one or more to stop by each evening, often leaving with pigeon or fish in their belly and sin on their conscience.

Gilbert spent each evening reading the works of the Greek philosophers and that of apostolics who lived before the rules of fasting and subservience had infused the monasteries of Germany. She tried to reconcile these early writings with the practices that were in place and realized that there was a choice of observance that she had not realized before. She tried to fashion a religion of her own, one that dealt with the reality of existence rather than traditions that were out of touch.

Henricus went along with her. He ate meat and fowl, fish and creatures of the sea, all in order to make this his home, a home that revolved around her. Such was his love and adoration that he lost part of himself to be with her. He adored her and no sacrifice was too big to make her happy.

Over time, the fame, wit, beauty, and learning of the young monk extended up and down the mountain and made its way into the city. Eventually the learned monks of Hymettus, the sellers of honey from their bees, visited the hut to discuss troublesome problems of dogma, demonology, and divination.

As happens, word spread and the bishop one day came to sit with Gilbert in the shade of a tree to talk with her. "How did it

Chapter Twenty-Two

happen that one as young as you, a novice, not quite twenty years has developed such a keen mind?" he asked.

Gilbert smiled. "I studied with Rabanus and he encouraged me. I am also quick to comprehend the texts and am honored that you have come."

"Your name is on everyone's lips. You have become the teacher of teachers. I know that priests, learned men, and magistrates have come to you to discuss matters of the mind and of the city."

"Yes. But rather than advice I offer possibilities to them, perhaps things they have not brought to their consciousness. I just liberate the ideas by talking to each. Nothing is set in stone. All is open to interpretation. I hope this pleases you," she said sincerely, almost as an afterthought. She did not want to fall out of favor with this man.

"I have received notice that some patricians from Rome will be arriving soon and they have asked to visit with those of learning. I am suggesting that this is something you should do. They are powerful and influential. If you impress them with the breadth of your knowledge, it may reach Rome."

"I seek not glory. I seek understanding. If it pleases you, I will be sure to take this opportunity. Thank you, bishop, for your support of my humble quest. I look forward to the encounter."

"One more thing before I leave. You are no longer a novice, so pick a name and I will elevate you to monk before you meet with them. What name do you wish to use?"

Gilbert thought, then spoke assuredly, thinking what was close to her real name, Agnes Johanna, "John. Father John. From now on that is the name I will use in my tracts."

chapter twenty-three

Henricus at first reveled in the attention his beloved gained from all who encountered her or sought her counsel. But he increasingly detected a detachment, a boredom with him as the circle of admirers and students grew and all whispered her name under their breath. Beneath his exterior of kindness and duty was a heart easily broken, and even a small cold look from her could cause him to fret and sulk. Replacing his placid exterior was a gloom and dread that made him jealous and suspicious of anyone who visited their hut. He began to follow her at a distance so that she would not know he trailed, seeing who she spoke with and where she sat, and as time passed, he began to anticipate the fateful day when she would no longer be his. He paid less attention to his appearance and forgot often to have nourishment that would sustain him as he sat for hours far enough away from her so as not to be seen.

Gilbert welcomed the Roman patricians with the same openness and candor she welcomed all who came to their home. These powerful men had traveled to secure support in Athens for their trade routes, and having heard about the learned monk were led to the hut one evening.

Gilbert and Henricus were seated at the table in front of their dwelling as the men approached. She looked up and did not recognize them, but she was always open to strangers. In fact, she was flattered and liked the attention she received.

Chapter Twenty-Three

Three men came near, and the first introduced the others. "I am Gustavos, he is Cesario, and the third, Maximus, recently arrived from Rome. We have heard of your reputation and are curious as to who inhabits the form of the one all speak of highly."

"Welcome. Please sit and we can clarify all matters for you."

Henricus looked up at her saying we, inferring that they both welcomed them and for once he would be included in the conversation, but Gilbert, now Father John, told him to go and get refreshments, forgetting even to proffer his name to the visitors.

He brought some fruit and savories and three cups to share their wine, pouring some into each. He laid the wine flask on the table with a thud. Gilbert by then was engrossed in a conversation about Rome. So he sulked off to a corner and sat fuming at the snub and at how quickly her attention to him could be diverted.

"We have come from Rome itself and were intrigued by the tales of the learned monk who writes tracts that are sold to those in the agora. Is this one of those?" asked Gustavos.

Gilbert looked at the papers in his hand and nodded, smiling at the man before her in his finery. "Yes. I wrote that one and these others," she said rising to get two others from inside and quickly returning without even a glance at Henricus.

"You write of matters of philosophy and theology, but I notice one of these is about rituals and practices of different sects," said Maximus. "Have you traveled so far at your age that you can write of these matters?"

"Yes. Originally from Mainz, I studied with Rabanus in Fulda for many years, and then traveled south to be part of this great and revered place of learning. I have encountered many different practices and rituals all in the name of God, and many who have forsaken the good works and teachings of our Lord and do harm to others."

"Specifically, what do you speak of?" Cesario said looking intently at the fair face and mannerisms of this man, so different in demeanor than anyone he had met before.

"There is much poverty, and many who are enslaved by pious men. Such is the custom of those who view the less desirable as tools for their labors. Taking the responsibility for the transportation of these to other owners, the slaves are moved about by merchant ships like produce and spices, traded in the flesh for material goods by those who are different in belief and have not accepted the one true God."

"Ah, yes. The French use those Jewish merchants to do their bidding in the transportation of slaves. But here in Athens do not the Byzantines take women for their harem from the breast of women who reared them? Is that not enslaving too?" asked Gustavos.

"They do. Where in the scriptures does it say to do that? Or is it really a question of who they enslave and who is of value to do their bidding?" Gilbert posed.

"In Rome there have always been those who were enslaved, heathens who do not accept the religion, and those we conquer that serve the aristocracy. Even the Pope has slaves," said another.

"Does that sanction the behavior? Does it have the blessing of the Pope? It is only a problem of economy, not of right or wrong as it should be," she said becoming so agitated that her cowling fell off her head as the men looked on her fair face.

This is an unusual monk, thought Maximus, *one of intellect and beauty. Too fair to be a boy, too learned to be a woman.*

"This other tract here says that those who till the soil are entitled to share in the profit of that work, even if they till the soil of others. A fair wage for the work, a fair share of the profits. Is this what you propose?"

Chapter Twenty-Three

"I merely have absorbed the work of Aristotle and others who advocate for being of this world and observing it, to treat all as a great experiment in the use of logic and deduction to solve the problems encountered. How to say a law or a rule is certain when no others have been tried or even thought of? Customs overtake thought mindlessly. To not use your thoughts and test your ideas seems anathema to me and only by educating the population can they be free and make choices of their own."

The three men looked at each other and back at Gilbert, marveling in the depth of her argument and the breath of her understanding of the way of the world.

After some time and glasses emptied repeatedly, the three thanked her for her counsel and bade farewell without even nodding to Henricus.

"We will think about your discourse and talk about you when we return. There are many in our land who would like to interact with you. Perhaps when they visit you will see them too," said Cesario.

"Of course. All are welcome at my door," and she turned smiling, leaving the cups for Henricus to clean up.

Pleased with herself, Gilbert prepared for bed. Henricus put away the drinking vessels and walked into the hut. He stared down at her on the mattress, his eyes burning, fighting to keep back the anger welling up in him, hands clenched at his sides.

She did not even look at him until he said, "Am I invisible? Have I not feelings and thoughts too? You treat me like the slaves you spoke of. You ignore me as a human being who is devoted to you, who led you to this place, who cared for your safety and keeps your secret." His voice rose in anger and became louder, and for the first time, he let go the suppressed feelings that he harbored about her treatment of him. She sat up and looked at him.

Unaware until this moment of the extent of his discontent, Gilbert blinked and rose, less in sympathy than in indifference. She stood and faced Henricus with finger pointed at him. "This is why we came. You consented to take me. It is not logical that now you would be angry about any of that. I have tolerated your moods, and, if you think I do not see when you follow me everywhere I go, you are mistaken. What do you think I am doing that you are jealous? I am teaching and selling my tracts, and talking with those who seek my words and taking in the words of those who have something to offer me." Her voice also got louder and neighbors started to gather outside to see what the commotion was. "You have no right to talk to me about any of this. If you do not like our situation, you are free to go elsewhere!"

Henricus was frozen in place. This had not occurred to him. She was telling him to accept the situation or leave. He expected an apology. He expected that she would relent and be made aware of her behavior. Instead he was the one on the defensive. He looked down at the dirt floor and lowered his voice as he stammered, "I could never leave you."

"Then do not expect me to change," she said turning to lie down on the pallet.

She fell asleep immediately, and he turned and walked outside. Curious passersby stood there not understanding how two monks could quarrel like a married couple. Henricus said, "Go on home. Just a misunderstanding. Not a problem."

They disbursed, but he overheard one woman say to another, "Could the other be his companion? I heard those monks do all sorts of ungodly things."

"Quiet, they will hear you. But yes, I thought the same thing. The other is just too pretty."

Henricus took a walk and came back and lay down next to

Chapter Twenty-Three

Gilbert. He placed one arm over her, and she hugged him in her sleep. *No,* he thought, *I can never leave her. I will just have to live through this. I will try to be more tolerant, but she will have to be more aware that I have needs too.*

By the time Henricus woke, Gilbert had already left for the day. He decided not to follow her and went off to tend to their plantings and do chores, later paying a visit to the monastery to reawaken the feelings he had when living in a protected place. *There is peace here. A tranquility that is good for the soul,* he thought.

Gilbert had two new tracts that she wrote as Father John, and she took a spot in the philosophy corner of the marketplace. Those who recognized her came over to talk and peruse her new writings. She thought little of the night before until later when she walked back to the hut and found a meal ready to share and Henricus already pouring the wine.

Without talking about it, they both ate. When they were finished, they went to bed early and made love, he out of genuine caring and deep feelings for her, and she out of necessity to calm his mind and quiet his tongue.

Chapter Twenty-Four

Calm prevailed in the household for some time. Henricus was somewhat content with the few crumbs of affection Gilbert bestowed on him, and she, oblivious to his distress, went about her routine of studying, writing, and selling her tracts in the agora.

Niketas, the bishop, came to visit often, and as her fame grew, he consulted with her on matters of significance to the Church and the advancement of its teachings. On one of her trips to the library to secure some reference for one of her tracts, he found her in the library and sat down next to her.

"Father John," he said in hushed tones so as not to disturb the others reading in the library.

She neither looked up nor acknowledged his presence so absorbed was she in the document before her.

"Father John," he uttered again, touching the arm holding the quill.

She looked up and blinked, slowly coming out of her reverie from being immersed in the topic she was researching.

"You are certainly single-minded my son. I was told you were here, and I wish to speak to you. Could we step outside for a moment?" She followed him reluctantly into the courtyard.

Gilbert was unaware of how unusual this was. As her fame grew, she outshone this humble man and when those in Athens sought advice, they usually came to her. For him to come to her

Chapter Twenty-Four

now rather than send some other to fetch her was out of order for someone as powerful as the bishop.

"Niketas, I am sorry not to respond sooner, but I was so absorbed in this topic for the new tract that I am unaware of anything except my mission." Gilbert was trying to appease him although she really would rather have just gone on working, and she glanced repeatedly back to the table where she sat just a few seconds before. In the few years she had been in Athens, she had outgrown his ability to engage her in meaningful dialogue about dogma. Niketas was no Rabanus. But as Henricus had said and she thought now, *I must be polite to him, after all he is our host here in Athens.*

"Father John, I have received notice that emissaries from the new Pope are coming from Rome. Evidently your dealings with the many Roman merchants that come here and have purchased your writings have reached the ears and eyes of Leo IV. He was recently unanimously selected as the new Pope by the Cardinals to succeed Sergius II. In fact, he has read some of your tracts carried back by the emissaries to the city. This is a great honor, or it could be a disaster, since on many matters you seem to agree, but on others you vehemently disagree with the pontiff."

"I think there is a logic of dialogue that I have acquired here that allows me to surpass the acceptable dogma. I use reason to question the efficacy and pertinence of certain beliefs. I would like to discuss some of the salient points with you. Could we sit down and do that now?" asked Gilbert.

"Father John, you are not listening to me." He was getting impatient. "I am cautioning you to be careful since the Pope's influence and power is growing and he can elevate or ruin you easily. You have a tongue that is acidic at times, and your impatience with others that do not see as you do is worn outwardly. This is not a trait you should advance, but one that you need to learn to hold in check."

Gilbert looked at him without expression. She was totally unaware that her demeanor could engender dislike or even hatred so absorbed was she in her work. "What do you mean Niketas? That I should not speak my mind? That is why I came here. That is my life work. I care not what others think, I only care for the quest of truth, like your Aristotle. What can be proven in matters of faith and practice in this world is my reason for study."

"As you have become an advisor for me, I am suggesting that you may have a future as that for Pope Leo someday. If that came to pass, the papacy is a den of intrigue and mystery among the cardinals and bishops and you have to learn to hold your tongue and listen to what others are saying in order to survive. Rome is a den of intrigue. The Pope is like a king there and he rules his followers as soldiers in a war. I am not saying this is your fate, only that I want you to be more aware of how others see you. To become more cognizant of yourself and the consequences of your actions and of your words."

Gilbert fell silent, an unusual condition for her. She had not thought about this at all. Care in hurting the feelings and sensibilities of others was long ago repressed. Her childhood had taught her to steel herself from those thoughts and accompanying behaviors. She made herself invisible then. She would have to sort this out for herself now if this was to go further and in fact she was to go to Rome someday.

"You mean this. I respect your advice and will think on this further. I appreciate the warning, and I will not say or do anything that would reflect badly on you or your province."

"I hope not. We in Athens are connected to Rome in many ways, both economically and spiritually. I would expect all who are

Chapter Twenty-Four

part of our Church to take to heart my words and present us well should the occasion arise."

Gilbert understood fully what he was saying. He was looking after her and himself and his people. *Could my work be so important to the Pope that he would summon me there? I have heard that he has more things pressing on his mind than a simple scholar in Athens. He behaves like a king fortifying the city from the invasion of the Saracens. And if he summoned me, would I be the emissary of the bishop or my own person, a poor monk from Mainz, who could make a contribution to the Church?* she thought.

"I assure you I will represent you well, Niketas. Calm your mind."

She turned as he did and went back to her research fully absorbed in what she was writing rather than further contemplating what he said.

Walking home, she returned to the conversation and decided that she would be more watchful from then on and register the reactions of others as she interacted with them. This was a skill she might need in the future. She decided to start with Henricus.

He was coming in from tending the plantings and watched her head toward the hut. She looked down as she walked, not ahead, lost in her own thoughts. Henricus was used to that. But this time, as she neared, she raised her head and noticed that he was looking at her, and she smiled. He tried to suppress his surprise, but his love for her made him smile back.

As they sat down to dinner on one evening when there were no visitors, Gilbert asked him, "What do you know of the new Pope, this Leo IV?"

"The monks have been telling tales of him, as they do, and I understand he was chosen unanimously. He is Roman and acts more like a king, a warrior, than a holy man."

"He is violent?" asked Gilbert.

"No, not violent—careful. I heard he is gathering workers, religious and nonreligious, to work on a wall to surround the papal area in case the Saracens invade. He is working on a strategy to rid Rome of the threat as did the Gauls."

"He is many talented?" she asked.

"So they say. Plans include the remaking of the gates to Rome and towers to defend the city, and he personally has scouted the area on foot and horseback to encourage the workmen and supervise the construction. All to stop the infidels from incursion into the city. He is a true Roman who loves his city and has vowed to defend its honor."

"He is a man of the cloth, they say, a holy man, who is of this world and the practicality of protecting the symbols of religion and a just way of life. He must be very learned to have mastered both the secular and religious."

"It is said. That is all I know. You can ask your next visitors from Rome when they come. I am sure they will further enlighten you."

"Niketas says that there may in fact be emissaries from the Pope coming. He must be seeking support for their endeavors."

"Ah. Then can we anticipate that they will make their way here? Or will you receive them with Niketas?" Henricus said spitefully.

His tone and words made Gilbert turn and look at him more closely. "Is there something you want to say to me, Henricus? I thought we were just having a discussion. But you seem perturbed and I do not like the implication." She spoke in a low voice so he had to pay attention to hear her.

They stared at each other for some time with him finally backing off and looking away.

She turned back to her meal, silently finished quickly, stood up,

Chapter Twenty-Four

and walked out of the hut. He cleared the table and walked out to her, sheepishly asking her to come back inside.

Turning, she looked at him with cold eyes. "I am going for a walk to clear my head. I will be back. What has happened to you, Henricus, that we cannot discuss our day without suspicion and mistrust creeping into our conversation? Ask and I will tell you truthfully anything you want to know, but do not talk to me again the way you just did." She turned and walked down the path to sit on a hill and watch the sunset alone.

The next day, Gilbert wrote the beginning of a new tract, one that she had been thinking about for some time. The main thesis was that the Church should temper their teachings and be more in alignment with the times in which they live. She used informed inquiry as the basis of her argument stating both sides equally. The first part was the value of a strict dogma, one adhering to the Church teachings and its mission to bring the word of God to the world. The other was that the dogmatic teachings had to be tempered with the practicality of living in the world and be adaptable to the issues and problems faced in reality. It was a call to alter the practices of the Church to better serve its followers and their way of life. Without making any judgment on her part, she fairly laid out her thesis and antithesis and set about making multiple copies of the essay to take to the agora when it was completed.

A few weeks later she sat in her usual spot and attracted many who sought her opinion and wanted to see her latest writings. From down the lane, she spotted two robed men who she did not recognize. They stopped by other vendors without buying their wares, asking each a question. Gilbert saw one point in her direction and watched the two men turn and look at her from afar. They headed for her, and Gilbert sat up a little straighter, looking down at her papers.

"Are you the monk, Father John, who sells religious tracts?"
Gilbert looked up at the finely robed men and nodded.
"What is your latest?" one asked.
She held up her latest one so they could peruse it.
"Whence have you come?" she asked.
"Rome. We are emissaries from the Pope here to talk to Niketas. He suggested we find you and see what you have produced that may be of interest to the Pope. So here we are at your service."
Gilbert tried to stay calm though her heart was elated that the attention of the Pope, at least through the emissaries, might signal the beginning of a new chapter in her life. She gave not a thought to how this would change for Henricus.

Chapter Twenty-Five

The next morning a messenger arrived at the hut. Henricus was already out, and Gilbert came to the door when he called her name.

"What may I help you with?"

"Niketas would like for you to join him this evening for dinner. He is hosting the Roman emissaries, and he believes this would be of interest to you. They have specifically asked that you join them."

"Henricus also?" she asked.

"No. They did not specify that he should come. Only you."

"I see. I will be there."

They left, and Gilbert, being independent in her actions, planned to leave Henricus a note that she was summoned to the abbey and would not be there for dinner. She gave no thought to him being left out.

"Henricus," she wrote, "Niketas has asked that I be present this evening for a meeting he has arranged. I will take nourishment there so there is no need to make a meal." There was nothing personal in the note, only the facts he needed to know.

She gathered some of her tracts for sale and went off to the agora planning to go directly to the abbey after she finished there. Since the number of buyers was sparse this day, she arrived early at the abbey and went once more to the library to look at a document she was using for a new tract. The subject of her new thesis was that belief, unwavering belief in the Church, was very hard to sustain. Therefore, the measures open are coercion, teaching, and conversion of nonbelievers. The path of the Church was clearly one of the three. Coercion led to violence, teaching was slow, but conversion was the acceptance of faith. It engendered true leadership and followership and was the most lasting of the choices, but it took the longest time of the three. That seed of an idea consumed her until someone came to get her for dinner.

Niketas sat at the head of the table with the two emissaries from the Pope on one side of him. He motioned for her to take the seat on the other side, facing the visitors. Other members of the abbey and some aesthetes from neighboring communities were also guests. Greek delicacies and Retsina wine were served, all of which Gilbert ate sparingly. Her glass was filled with a wine she preferred, which Niketas had remembered. She was also served less spiced dishes that were more to her simple tastes and upbringing.

"Tell us how goes the building program in Rome. We hear that the Pope is busy fortifying the Church of Saint Peter with walls," said Niketas.

"Yes. He is determined to shore up the area afflicted by the excesses committed by the Saracen soldiers and like a good Roman, he dreads their return," said the emissary.

"A wise move on his part."

"He is basically executing the design of Leo III to build a new town around Saint Peter's. The foundations already have started. This is to ensure the safety of all," said the second papal representative.

"And how does he expect to afford such an undertaking?" asked Gilbert.

The two men turned to look at her with surprise.

"Do you think the Pope has not thought of these things?"

"Yes. But I am curious as to the alliances he has made to ensure

Chapter Twenty-Five

covering the costs of materials and labor. That is all. I am not questioning the practicality of such an undertaking, just as to the means to achieve it. The good Pope seems to have his hand much in the secular of Rome, which I understand is his birthplace. Is this at the expense of the religious or does it advance that agenda in some way?"

Niketas turned to Father John, fire in his eyes, that he would question the purpose of the Pope, knowing that these two would take back her comments to his Holiness.

"We have your answer. The Pope has engaged Emperor Lothaire who has sent contributions of all his brothers as well as himself. Many pounds of silver arrive daily, and the Pope has assembled Roman builders. For labor, neighboring towns have sent workmen employed by the public or the monasteries to work on the task. The plans have been drawn up, and they are underway, starting with the wall of Rome that had fallen in ruin."

"So they are first protecting the city in order to protect the Church. Am I correct?" said Gilbert.

"Yes. And the Pope is most aware that this is the first task to make the Church strong. In order to do the work of God there has to be a Rome to direct the flock."

"It seems Leo is determined to assert papal independence. Did he not forsake Lothair's approval to be consecrated Pope?" asked Gilbert.

"True, but they both understand that they have to unite to stave off the Saracens, and a strong protective wall and alliance with the Pope is good for all," Niketas said.

"The next task is to rebuild the gates, and build fifteen towers from the foundation to the roof, and each day, sometimes on foot and sometimes on horseback, he rides out to encourage the workmen that they labor for the Lord." The second emissary added,

"Protecting the image of the Pope as one who not only is wise, and leads, but is also doing the work of the Lord."

"And to protect them from invasion of the infidels," added the other.

"So he is a king as well as a Pope defending his realm and protecting the Church from false dogma. I raise my glass in his honor," said Gilbert trying to appease Niketas and soothe the emissaries.

During the rest of the dinner, Niketas tried to steer the conversation away from argumentative subjects. He wanted the emissaries to take back a good impression of his abbey and the people of Athens, and he thought Gilbert understood this and would help put him in the good graces of the Pope.

Gilbert, wrapped up in her own world, thought little of others, and, like Henricus, Niketas had outgrown his usefulness to her. She increasingly became interested in Rome itself and the next seat of learning.

The rest of the dinner was less caustic, and by the time she left, Niketas relaxed enough to be a gracious host to all. At the end of the dinner, the emissaries rose and thanked Niketas. "We will bring your good wishes to the Pope, and we thank you for the feast of delicacies that we have just enjoyed."

"You are most welcome," said Niketas, "and I hope that the relations between Athens and Rome will continue and become fruitful in the deliverance of the word of God to the world."

As they left the abbey, the two Romans walked out with Father John. She walked, back straight, head high, and headed on the path toward her home but was called back by the emissaries who walked faster to catch up and talk to her.

"Wait young Father John," one called.

She turned, standing in the moonlight on the quiet land, and waited for them to catch up.

Chapter Twenty-Five

"We enjoyed the conversation with you and reading your tracts. I think you are a forward-looking scholar and that the Pope would be interested in speaking to you. If you have any others we could bring back, we would be grateful to take them too. The Pope too is an innovator and we have been told to look for others who he might use for consultation. Do you have plans to travel to Rome? We could arrange for an audience for you."

"To Rome? I had not thought about that. I came here from Fulda to study and learn. That is my interest. I write my tracts to earn some money to sustain my studies. Nothing more."

"Well, we think that you should consider more. Pope Leo is always looking to expand his knowledge too, to find others to consult with as he innovates and tries to expand the influence of the Church. We would like to take all your writings to him to read and then it is up to the two of you whether there is interest in his part and in yours to situate yourself closer to Rome."

Gilbert, for the first time in her life, was without words. What would this mean to her present situation, to the years of study, to the years of travel, to her advancement in the Church? She actually viewed herself as a humble monk and her secret was so repressed that the practicality of keeping her real gender from others was an afterthought. She only was cognizant of what this opportunity would bring to her. Not what the consequence would mean for Henricus and his devotion to her.

Coming out of her reverie, she said, "Yes. There are other essays. I am working now on an interesting one. It should be done soon. Then I could copy it for you to carry back with others that I have."

"That would be good. We leave in a few days. Might we stop by your place in the agora say in three days' time and you can deliver them to us to take back to his Holiness."

"Yes. I will collect them and have them ready for you."

They bowed in the Roman manner and turned walking back to the abbey where they were staying.

Gilbert walked slowly back to the hut and Henricus. She had work to do over the next two days and wanted to complete the new tract for them to take with them. She thought it was the best she had written and would provoke much discussion, especially if read by the Pope.

Henricus was already asleep when she got back. She lay down with her back turned to him, her thoughts far away, imagining the Pope reading her tracts. Henricus, sensing her presence, turned and saw that she was immersed in her thoughts that did not include him so he turned his back toward hers and slept fitfully in dread that she was moving increasingly further away from him.

Gilbert woke early before Henricus and, without a word, went out with her notes to the library at the monastery to complete her current tract. By the end of the morning she was done, so she returned home to make copies of this document and that of others she wished the emissaries to take with them to Rome.

Working at the rustic table, her fingers covered in ink, she wrote diligently for two days, leaving off only when Henricus urged her to take a break and eat for sustenance.

By the third day she was done and, waking early, gathered up all the tracts and set off to the agora to meet the emissaries before they sailed back to Rome.

They came in the afternoon before returning to the vessel that would leave on the first outgoing tide. She had bundled the tracts in cloth wrapped with twine. As they approached, there were others who were looking at her documents, and they waited patiently as she spoke to one with complete attention to the gist of the argument.

Talking off to the side, one of the emissaries said quietly, "He

Chapter Twenty-Five

is most skilled in the dialogic, I think. He takes each idea and can see both sides before logically coming to a conclusion as he argues points of conjecture."

"Yes. He would be a perfect foil for the Pope. He enjoys this give and take and logic of discussion, and he welcomes diverse ideas," said the other emissary.

"I think we will be back to convince him to come with us next time."

Gilbert, finished with the last customer, looked up at the two and smiled. She reached down and took out of her bag the neatly wrapped package to give to them. Standing, she looked at the package and held it out to one of the two. "I hope that your travels are uneventful and your trip here was successful."

"Thank you. We leave later today and must go to the boat now. Father John, we will be back. I am sure. If all goes well, I believe that the Pope will be interested in meeting you. While we are away, please consider carefully what a summons from Pope Leo would mean for you. We will be in touch to let you know of his reaction."

"I am honored just to have him read what I have written," she said modestly.

"And to know your name, Father John. This will follow and you must prepare yourself for travel."

She nodded and bowed back at them, watching as they made haste to get on the sailing vessel.

She packed up her wares and walked up to the Acropolis to look out over the city. She scanned over the antiquities and glanced over to the harbor where her work was being taken to the Pope and smiled.

Heading home, she knew she had to face Henricus. She would have to prepare him carefully if she decided to move on. Leaving him was less of a misfortune for her than it was for him.

Do not jump to conclusions before anything has happened, she thought. *Behave as usual until there is something to tell him that is certain.*

In her heart she knew he would be devastated, especially if she wanted to go alone and leave him, finally, behind.

chapter twenty-six

No one came from the Pope. Gilbert went about her tasks of writing and selling tracts and Henricus went about his of planting and reaping, taking care of their hut, and fretting about his love.

The night she came home from giving the Roman emissaries her tracts, Henricus was distraught at her absence, not knowing where she was. He left the hut not to return for two days. By morning, it was raining so hard that Gilbert did not go out. She scrounged in the bins for something to eat. Henricus was the one who cooked; Gilbert hadn't cooked since the days she was tyrannized by her stepmother, and, if left on her own, she surmised, she would starve to death. *He is good for that and for comfort, but I no longer can discuss my work with him nor can I share the possibility that awaits me if catching the eye and ear of the Pope.*

He returned two evenings later, wet and coughing from staying out in the elements.

"Why did you not go to the monastery and keep yourself out of the elements?" she asked, boiling water to make an herbal tea for him and motioning for him to go nearer the warmth of the fire.

"What difference does it make? Did you come to find me? Did you notice I was not here?"

"Please, Henricus. Not now. Just take the wet cloak off and rid yourself of the chill."

He grunted as she struggled to remove the wet cloak and hang it near the fire to dry as he lifted one weary arm, then the other. His cough was deep in his chest, and he was very tired, too tired to sip the tea. He only wanted to lie down and rest.

Henricus slept fitfully and she sat in the corner reading and making sure the fire did not die down and chill him further. By morning he was shivering, but she nursed him for days until his fever stopped and his coughing subsided somewhat. It lingered for weeks, never completely gone.

Their lives together went on for many months just as it did before. Gilbert did not even have Niketas to counsel her since he was summoned to Constantinople and did not return for some time. When he finally came back to Athens and she sought an audience with him to ask about the Pope, he told her, "The Pope is engaged in fighting off the Saracens who have sights on Ostia, the port of Rome. He was there for the battle."

"The Pope fights. Such a modern Pope who is of the people this Leo is," she said to Niketas.

"There is more. He used the Church wealth to repair the walls, built towers, and stretched chains across the Tiber to defend Rome. He even armed the militia using his funds and convinced the inhabitants of Gaeta, Amalfi, and Naples to help defend Ostia. He personally visited all the posts and blessed the troops in a mass. He is a Roman defending his city, and he engenders the idea that the republic is to be fought for. But he also is protecting the Christian people like a king who watches over his subjects."

"Remarkable. Did the Pope's troops prevail?"

"Yes. The pirate ships appeared and the Neapolitan galleys led the way to engagement. Then a storm divided the Muslims, and the Christian ships returned to port. The scattered Saracens lost many ships and others grounded, and when the storm was over, the Arab fleet was picked off and many prisoners were taken."

Chapter Twenty-Six

So this is why no one has returned here, she thought.

"What occupies the Pope now, I cannot imagine," said Gilbert.

"I hear he is intent on protecting St. Peter's Basilica. He is now enclosing the area with walls and restoring the basilica, replacing its gold covering that was stolen and is now studded with precious gems."

"He is making sure that this does not happen again, I presume," said Gilbert.

"Yes. He is appealing to all the Christian kingdoms to confront the Arab raiders and keep them away for good."

"Let us pray that he succeeds," she added.

"Be patient, my young friend. I know your meeting with his emissaries was fruitful, and they took their impressions and your work back to Rome."

She smiled at him, realizing that he was fully aware of the possibility that she would be summoned to Rome. "Yes, I will try to be," she replied.

Henricus never got over his lingering cough, no matter what Gilbert did to stop it. She brought herbs to the hut and made poultices and teas, but it remained present, often waking her at night. After eight years in Athens and nearing thirty years of age, she was familiar with all the manuscripts and inhabitants so that the city was as insipid as Henricus's lamentations. She was ready to move on, consumed with a desire to broaden her knowledge once again and to spread her thoughts in a broader venue. Growing impatient with the routine of everyday life in Athens, she roamed the streets contemplating what to do about Henricus who never really recovered from his affliction of mind and body. His strength waned over the next few months, making him an invalid unable to perform even the routine tasks of tending the garden and preparing meals without fits of coughing that were often bloody.

While walking one evening near the beach, after bidding Niketas goodbye prior to his return to Constantinople, she saw in the harbor a foreign vessel whose sails were making way to port. She walked hurriedly to better view the ship and saw that it was Italian.

After the ship docked at the port, Gilbert approached and spoke to the sailors in Latin. "For what purpose has this boat come here, kind sir?"

"This vessel belongs to the bishop of Genoa, William the Little. It is on a mission to procure frankincense. We head back toward Rome tomorrow to deliver our cargo."

This is my chance to get to Rome, thought Gilbert.

"Would you be averse to letting me join you on your short journey? I desire to go to the papal city."

The sailor thought for a moment and, realizing the ship had a need for a monk on board, said, "In truth we have a requirement for a chaplain. Ours was swept away standing in the prow trying to quell the waves by throwing consecrated bits into the sea."

"I would be willing to step into his place and fulfill his obligations for safe passage to Rome," she answered.

"Let me take this to the captain. Wait here."

The sailor came back and told her, "Prepare for the journey and be at the dock at dawn. We will not wait for you to appear. If you are here, we will transport you to your destination."

She returned home to find Henricus moving about the hut. Sometimes, before the end of life, there is a rallying of mind and spirit, and he was determined not to take his leave of her as yet.

"Henricus, you are up and about. Are you feeling better?"

"Somewhat. I seem to be breathing a little easier today."

"That is good," she said a little distractedly.

Chapter Twenty-Six

"Come with me to the cave tonight where we can be alone and dine and sleep in each other's arms. Please, Gilbert. It has been too long that we were alone in that special place."

"Of course. I will meet you at dusk. I have to go out for a little while. Are you sure you are up to this?"

"I want to do this." His pale face looked at her as he stifled a cough.

She thought this over and realized it was important to him to make an effort. "I will be there."

Gilbert went out to make her preparations for the trip. She actually thought that if Henricus was up to it, she would take him with her, assured that two monks on the trip would certainly not be a problem. She had gathered her tracts and put them in a bag, along with her books of most importance while Henricus was distracted preparing the supplies for their dinner. Taking her belongings to the boat, she reassured the sailor that she would be back in time for departure.

As she approached the grotto near the harbor, she heard the rasp of his cough before she entered. He was sweaty and weak, shivering as she entered the cave, but yet he had prepared dinner and was stoking a fire to keep warm.

"Sit by the fire and dry your cloak. It is wet from the waves," he said motioning her to a rock. She saw that he had prepared piles of straw to better cushion them for the night in a corner near the fire.

Gilbert was not hard-hearted. She had been with Henricus since she was eleven, never separated, and had loved him and cared for him, but now she only felt he was a burden. She did not want to abandon him still, but he was ill and could not be expected to live much longer. She thought, *He is rallying one more time, making this grand gesture at reconciliation, but his illness will take over soon and I know this is a temporary state. I cannot risk what little life he has left on a voyage. And I need to go alone on the rest of my journey.*

They ate, and he grew increasingly weaker, so she lay him down on the straw and cradled his head, rocking slowly until his fit of coughing ceased and he fell asleep. He awoke in the middle of the night and thought, *She loves me still,* as he looked into her face for one last time before he closed his eyes.

Henricus's breath came heavy and rasped with an echo in the cave. She rocked him all night. By dawn he lay unconscious in the arms of his love. She knew he could not rally for the journey and that this would be his last day.

Gilbert carefully covered him and realized she had to leave for the boat immediately or she would miss its sailing. Finding a young shepherd up at that early hour she pleaded that he go to the cave and tend to the dying monk. Giving him money and instructions, she turned and raced to the dock, and, as the sailboat drew away from the port, she looked back to where her love was and whispered, "God speed, my Henricus. Rest in peace."

Chapter Twenty-Seven

Gilbert sat on the deck of the sailing vessel bound from Athens to the port of Ostia, Italy. Over the nearly 500 nautical miles, approximately two weeks of sailing, she had time to contemplate the events of the past months. With little to do aboard, and calm seas ahead, she was left with her own thoughts. The captain did not need her to cast trinkets in the water to keep it calm or to pray with an ailing crew member. She had little to occupy her mind after reading and rereading her tracts to see if they were really worthy of an audience with the Pope.

She wrapped her cloak around her and stared out to sea, pensively being introspective, possibly for the first time in her life. She thought about the events of the past few days, of the months when Henricus had been so demanding of her that he was driven to make himself ill. Gilbert did not feel responsible for causing his death, but she did regret that their relationship was not better at the end, enough so that he would have the option of going with her on the next journey to Rome. *But,* she thought, *did I really want him anymore? Did I really want him to come along?*

She tried to push those thoughts from her mind, to create reasons why he would have been better off staying, had he been given that choice. Had he not died as she was looking toward the next part of her education? She tried in vain to make him well using all that she knew, but when he came home his ailment was too far advanced. Wandering in the elements made him ill, that and his innate jealousy that drove him to be reckless. Had she not been so selfish, perhaps none of that would have happened? But he always knew what she wanted and supported her unconditionally. Until the end when he changed. She was the constant, always knowing what she was about.

It was not to be, she thought, *poor soul, driven by love for me. What did I do to him? I could not stop him from being irrational, jealous, and demanding of my time. I could not stop my work and fawn on him.* Realizing she was making excuses, she fell into deep thought about what she had lost and how for the first time in her life she was alone, really alone.

He was my love, my first love. He helped make me into this monk, this guise that the world sees, a disguise because it is forbidden for me to be open. I am grateful, I am proud to have known someone so true who cared for me as no other will ever. Her inner dialogue went from irritation to admiration as she shared these thoughts with no one.

So she continued with this talk as they sailed from Athens south, then west across the Ionian Sea. Up ahead she could see the Strait of Messina as the vessel made its way through the waterway, land on either side of her as the ship inched its way up the west coast of Italy. It would take a day more to reach Ostia, the port at the mouth of the Tiber just thirty kilometers from Rome.

Reaching the port, she was the first ready to get off the sailing vessel. "Thank you for taking me on this leg of your journey. I hope I was of some service to you as it was smooth sailing and I was not called on too often to aid the crew."

"Perhaps your presence was fortuitous, Father John, and that is why the seas were calm and all went well. There are many small vessels at the port to take you up the Tiber to Rome," said the captain.

Gilbert nodded and disembarked. She found a small means

Chapter Twenty-Seven

of transport, a boat taking supplies to Rome, and she asked for passage. Amidst live chickens and grain, she stood for most of the journey as the supply boat made its way up the ancient river.

Debarking, she walked slowly around the hills surrounding Rome as she made her way to St. Peters.

In Rome, Pope Leo was preparing for the coming Synod now that the Saracen threat was mollified and his city protected by strong walls and gates. A Benedictine monk himself, he was laying out the rules for the clergy that reflected the ethics of the time and his background. The edicts he wrote included rules for strengthening the priesthood and included a ban on priests engaging in drinking alcohol or attending dog races or bird fights or entering pubs. *The lax rules of previous Popes and usual practices of the priesthood,* he thought, *had to be unsung,* so he included a mandate that the priests must wear clerical dress to distinguish them from the others in the city. When presiding at weddings, priests should refrain from taking part in the bacchanalia of celebrations, and they should know the prayers of Mass and psalms by heart.

His thoughts on women were equally strict. He banned women from approaching the alter and touching the chalice because he distrusted women. They also could not sing in church. Yet, he opened a monastery for women where, under his fatherly protection, the chosen novices entered the Church.

It was into this atmosphere Father John came, deciding en route to forsake Gilbert forever and rename herself to all. Her first day in the city, there was some sort of festival to Saturnalia in honor of the ancient gods. Bands of drunken Christians danced to profane songs; such was the state of Rome. The splendor of the edifices, long gone and plundered by Charles the Great, adorned a church in France, and the churches of Leo's predecessors were a melee of Roman and Oriental artifice.

She spent the first days in Rome wandering about the city, and understood that Leo would now have to turn his attention to the population who needed to be instructed in the true teachings of the Church if they were to be saved. *His task is large*, she thought. *Perhaps there is a place for Father John in this undertaking.*

Her audience with the Pope came soon after her arrival.

Father John slowly walked into the Pope's presence with her head bowed and humbled. Leo was imposing but quickly offered, "Come my son. Take a seat so we may better acquaint ourselves with each other."

Laid out on the table was one of her tracts delivered, she supposed, by the emissaries that came to Athens. Leo picked it up and said, "Welcome to Rome. I trust your travels have been easy and without incident."

"Yes, it was easy crossing and the seas were calm."

Leo held the tract up to her and said, "I have read this and others you have scribed. You are most skilled and learned, and I find the tone of your theses most intriguing. You recommend some radical changes to the way we think about the subject."

"Thank you. I just worked through the problem as I saw it and provided some recommendations to make changes for the better; changes that were more logical and in line with the changing times we live in."

"The times we live in. I assume you have walked through Rome and are aware of the issues of faith that are permeating this area. The people are not singular in the way that they believe nor in the manner in which the Church supports them so that they may lead a pious good life," said Leo.

"Yes, there is much to work on here. The people are more interested in gaining wealth and gaining superiority over each other and the world than they are in questions of theology. The

Chapter Twenty-Seven

old gods are present along with the one true God, and they are wont to give up the bacchanalia of the heathen life. Even the ancient statues reflect a message I am not sure the Church wants to perpetuate."

"Exactly, you are most perceptive to have picked up on those things so quickly, but we are making progress slowly and need great minds like yours to help in this endeavor. I have assured their safety from the Saracens, and now I need an army to save their minds and souls."

"I am at your service. I will do whatever you need me to do in order to bring the message of God to those here in Rome. I am your servant."

After an hour-long talk, the Pope looked at Father John and said, "I would like to give you an opportunity to extend your work and thoughts by making you a Professor of Theology at the College of Saint Martin, where Augustine himself formerly taught."

"Thank you. I am very grateful for your support and for this honor. It is what I have worked for, to be able to teach, study, and further my understanding of the Church and of how to bring the words of God to the world."

Pope Leo stood and walked Father John to the door. "It was most pleasant to meet the author of these tracts. Know I will be in touch with you from time to time to see how your work progresses. My blessings to you."

Father John smiled and nodded, then went through to the outer room, jubilant that she had found favor with Pope Leo and been given the opportunity to share her thoughts with others at the College of Saint Martin.

She walked through to the open area in front of St. Peters and looked up to the area where she had met with the Pope.

"A wise and learned man," she said out loud to no one in particular, only feeling the need to say it. "He has much to teach me, and hopefully I will serve him well."

Head held high, Father John walked off toward Saint Martin where she would assume the responsibility of teaching others with the sanction of the Pope.

Chapter Twenty-Eight

Father John walked from the meeting with the Pope directly to Saint Martin on Viale del Monte Oppico stopping on her way to retrieve the items she brought from Athens: books and tracts of her own work. This small edifice, built in the fourth century, was recently renovated by Pope Leo so that the interior reflected the splendor of the Church. Each of the two wings were receiving the last of the mosaics that the Pope ordered along with the almost completed frescoes. Father John stood admiring the work of the artisans and walked closer to the apse that bore an inscription also ordered by Leo. It read:

> Sergious the bishop began this house which you see, but he died and could not ornament it. However, when Pope Leo IV inherited the dignity of the throne of Rome he was touched by divine love and finished it better than it had begun, and decorated all of it with holy images. Also he founded a holy monastery and placed monks there who may be able to perform assiduous praises to the Lord. By such gifts may he be able to ascend to the heavenly kingdom, where Martin exultant and the holy Sylvester shine and rejoice together with the leader Christ. Because of the good deeds of them these famous temples shine.

A monk approached Father John, having already been informed

that a new leader was to take over the duties of head of the monastery and the church here at Saint Martin.

"Welcome, I am here to welcome our new abbot. My name is Father Amatus. I am to show you around the grounds and the monastery. I see you already have admired the beautiful artwork the Pope has placed in the apse. We are very proud that he has taken an interest in us."

"Thank you, Amatus. Pope Leo certainly is making improvements here, I see. And the inscription shows that he knows the significance of the history of this place. I hope that I am worthy of carrying out our mission and serve the Pope and the people under our care."

"Come. Let me take you to the monastery building and your quarters and office. You will meet all the others at dinner this evening. We hope you will lead us in prayers."

"Certainly I will." Father John followed Amatus, smiling to herself because this was exactly what she had hoped for. Eager to settle in and get to work, she followed him to her room and said, "Please, I would like to go directly to the office I will occupy and prepare for this evening. I will just leave this bag here and return once you show me the route."

"You are eager to begin," Amatus said with surprise in his inflection.

Father John thought, *That is what I am here for. I fear this monk has been taking things too easily since their abbot left the earth and I am a replacement who needs to reorganize and assert authority concerning the work and responsibilities of each monk if we are to succeed.*

"I assume you will introduce me to each of our monks at dinner. I would like a list of each of their names and what their duties are brought to my office before dinner. That is still hours away so you should have ample time."

Chapter Twenty-Eight

"Yes, Father John," said Amatus who had thought that showing Father John about the grounds would not be very taxing.

Every monastery is like a small city, and the monks, when they can, gossip. By the time the list was delivered to Father John, all the monks knew that changes were on the way. Looking over the list prepared by Amatus, each monk's name was followed by their chores along with the weekly schedule for serving the poor and teaching classes to the few people who attended. *Many of these will have to be changed if we are to attract people to this church.*

Before Vespers, Father John was escorted by Amatus to the church. The monks were all in attendance, waiting for the ritual of Vespers to begin. Each looked up at the young Father who would lead them. Walking slowly to the pulpit, and used to the rituals taught by Rabanus in Fulda, the traditional prayers were started and spoken from memory by Father John, who did not even need to open a book to recite them.

Each of the monks stared openly at Father John, impressed in the command of the service and in the manner in which he held their attention. When the formal service was over, Father John spoke saying, "I look forward to meeting with each and every one of you in the next days so that we can talk about the work before us. I am honored to be given this position by Pope Leo, and I have pledged to him to live up to the historical significance of having had Saint Augustine himself teach here. Let us dine together now and begin our journey."

Walking down from the pulpit, she searched out Amatus and nodded to him that she would follow to the dining hall where he led her to a front table facing the monks who sat communally at smaller tables. No one spoke, as was the custom in monasteries, but Father John suspected that this was not the usual for these men. *I will have to be harsh at first to get all in order if I am to succeed.*

Returning to her room, exhausted from the day, Father John washed and lay down on the cot provided. Falling into a deep sleep, the bell for early prayers at 4:00 a.m. woke her, and the first full day of leading this church began.

By midday she had met with almost all of the monks, discerning their strengths and weaknesses, and either maintained them in their position or reassigned them to other tasks. Her primary goal was to get more of the peasants involved in the Church and teach their children so that they would carry on the work of the abbey. A few of the monks were literate enough to be useful to her in her work. She selected one for her private secretary. He was the brightest, and his interview was far deeper in theology than the others.

"Where are you from, Dominic? Where did you study to be a monk?"

"I am not from Rome, but from a small village to the north. I ran away from home as a boy before I was cast out of my parent's home. They had too many to feed, and by nine, I was expected to make my own way. I found a merchant willing to take me to Rome where I thought I might find work, but when I got here, the only place I could find to accept me was this monastery. I gladly accepted and was taught the ways of life of the monks and the Church here and have lived within these walls since."

"You can read and write, I presume?" Father John in previous interviews encountered at least three other monks who could not.

"Yes. I can. The eyesight of the previous abbot was failing for some time, and he used me to read and write his correspondence. It was a great honor to serve him."

"I would like to make you my assistant. You will work with me and carry out my wishes. That includes implementing the revised schedule of chores for each of the monks. I am almost done with the interviews and will give you the new job assignments tonight.

Chapter Twenty-Eight

We will inform everyone after dinner of when and where they are to report tomorrow for work."

Dominic's handsome face was grim. "What is it?" asked Father John.

"They will not be happy. I think we must give them a rationale for the changes, to make them more palatable."

"Yes. I will. First to you I can say that our mission is to serve the people after God. To do that, the old pagan worship must be replaced with the message we have to deliver. I want the Church to be seen as benevolent and a place of refuge, to be a place to discuss life as it is and life in the hereafter. I have a plan to do that. I need your help to implement the plan."

"I think you need to pander to their baser interests before they will accept the rest of our theology."

"That is exactly what I intend to do."

After dinner, Father John stood and bade the monks remain in their seats.

"I have met with you all today and have made some decisions about elevating Saint Martin to the level it should be in the Church and in the community of people we can serve. First, there will be new assignments posted outside the door to the dining room for you to look at, and starting tomorrow, you are to report to each of them for work. I have discerned your individual strengths and hope that you will approach the new jobs with the same enthusiasm that I have undertaken mine. I have asked Father Dominic to be my assistant, and any questions you have can be addressed to him and he will convey them to me. A response will come in a timely fashion."

The monks all were looking from Father John to their neighbors, each with an air of disgruntlement that their routines were to be disrupted.

"Please know that our mission here is to teach our flock, and we will do that by whatever means we have. Those assigned to teaching duties for adults and children will be under my direction. I want this church to be a place where problems of life are either solved or comforting to our flock. I personally will meet with you tomorrow morning to begin the planning of a new teaching perspective, one more relevant to their lives. I have faith that you will embrace your new assignments and know that I am accessible and will be a participant fully in the works of this abbey. Thank you for making me feel welcome."

Father Dominic took the list from Father John and posted the assignments on the outer wall. For each change, there was at least one monk who remained in his position so as to teach the others what to do. The master of the kitchen remained while helpers were rotated to other jobs.

Father John, head held high, back erect, walked out of the dining room and headed to bed. Father Dominic was left to orderly dismiss the monks so they could find their name on the list. The few that could not read, he helped. In silence, the monks went to their cells to ready for the coming day.

chapter twenty-Nine

Within a month Father John had transformed the operation of the monastery and, fully confident, ventured immediately into the community surrounding Saint Martin trying to convince the people to come to services and to send their children to the school. Thinking long and hard about what to say to them so that they would attend, Father John decided that to dwell on scriptures at first was the wrong way to approach the task. Visiting them in their homes would generate a core of students who then could grow with the tales they told to others.

These people need more practical lessons, ones that could alleviate some of their hardships and make them comfortable coming to the abbey for nurturance, both spiritually and bodily. No religious dogma to begin, but practical information that could enlighten them to a better life. Who better than to do that than me? Father John. Anyone can change. The best place to start is with the children and make them literate. It opens the mind and the rest follows, she thought.

Father John gathered the literate monks and set before them a plan for lessons, not of scripture but of life, taught with pamphlets of her making: stories of planting and rotating crops, of cooking with different herbs and plants in the area, and of cleanliness and care for one's body to ward off disease. The children took the stories home, and slowly, some parents started to attend and the classes grew. For sermons, Father John would take a theme from scriptures and, by the end of a long sermon, transform the stories into practical tales and end them with hints for healthy cooking. Often, as time progressed, Pope Leo would attend these sermons and sit in the back, marveling at the breadth of knowledge and flexibility of this young Father to hold the attention of the flock. In a time of illiteracy, even with monks, this was a welcome sight.

On one such occasion Pope Leo approached Father John, saying, "You certainly have done remarkable work here in such a short time. You have loyal followers and your implementation of innovation is most appreciated. I only wish others had your skills so that all over Rome there would be pockets of learning going on such as this."

"I am your humble servant," Father John replied. "Please come and see our classes for children if you have the time. They learn all manner of practical arts, and Aristotle's mathematics and logic. It should prove most useful in modernizing the children who then can help their parents at home."

Father John was flattered by Leo's attention and slowly started to realize that there was more to aspire to. He thought, *I walk around the city and no one suspects that I am a charlatan. I have transformed myself so completely into Father John that I think of myself as such. I am seen by others as an innovator, a learned man. My cowling reveals only my nose as I walk, and no one questions my veracity. I am not a woman. I have changed my sex. Without Henricus, I do not even desire men. I hardly even think about him anymore. What is it I do want? I want the abbot's cloak, the legate's mule, the bishop's mitre. Perhaps even the Pope's golden shoes. Am I being too ambitious? I think not.*

For two years Father John worked at Saint Martin, teaching, writing, and flattering the influential who came to hear him speak or converse solely for advice. Father John composed hymns to

Chapter Twenty-Nine

Christ and to the Pope, the first to do so in Rome. He also practiced medicine at the abbey, and those who came to get healed were asked to participate in the classes in return.

Pope Leo was advancing in years and suffered from rheumatism. When he visited Saint Martin, Father John would give him herbs to have brewed into soothing teas, but Leo was tired. He knew that those around him could not take up some of the tasks he required because they were not educated enough to understand the intricacies of the mixture and nuance of politics and scripture.

Summoned to Pope Leo's private apartment to minister to a particularly bad bout of rheumatism, Father John was in awe. Leo sat on a throne of purple and gold surrounded by vases made of silver and golden goblets, and jeweled finery adorned him. Father John knelt on one knee and shut his eyes, so dazzled by the splendor around him. *I grew up in such humble surroundings, among Benedictine monks, then in huts of poverty. This is not real to me*, she thought.

Kissing the Pope's shoes, he rose up and Pope Leo bade Father John to sit next to him.

"I have brought you herbs for your pains and a salve for your hands. I think this might help." Father John held out the mixture for Leo to pat on his red and gnarled fingers.

"The tea mixture is different than the last time. Can someone bring hot water in a flask so it can brew?"

Pope Leo motioned to one of his aides, and as he sipped, Father John made ready to leave.

"Stay, my boy. I enjoy our conversations and it will take my mind away from weighty matters."

"At your pleasure."

They talked of theology for some time when one of the Pope's assistants entered and approached. "I have prepared the document you asked for. You should read it and sign so it can be sent by messenger."

Leo creased his brow and frowned as he read. "You have missed the point entirely. This is not what I meant to say. Must I do everything by myself?"

He looked at Father John who was taking in the conversation and handed the document to him. "I wanted the message to alert the estate holders that we will be taxing their property according to acreage, not as a tithe but as a direct method to make the amount fair. That is not what it says!"

Father John went over to the desk and took up quill and ink and started writing and editing the document. After completing and rereading it, he handed it over to Leo who did the same.

"Perfect. Rewrite this and send it out please," he said to the assistant. "A rather delicate message needs a lighter touch, a more tactful approach. You understood that immediately."

Father John nodded, secretly lauding himself for being able to do exactly what the Pope wanted. Leo stared at him for a long time and a glint of his eye told Father John that he was up to something concerning him.

"My boy, I am in need of someone who can help me on a daily basis. Someone smart and quick to understand what I want and how I want it to be communicated to others. I am getting older and really there is no one in these walls who can do that. But you and I seem to have a quick understanding of each other and therefore you can anticipate well what it is I want."

It took all her courage not to jump up for joy in the Pope's presence as she immediately understood what an opportunity this would be to enter the inner circle of the Pope's confidants. This was the route that lay before her, and, she thought, *How far can this lead? To the papacy itself?*

Chapter Twenty-Nine

"I would like for you to be my private secretary. To begin immediately. Is there someone you have trained who can continue the good work at Saint Martin? I do not want that to regress, but to be a shining example of what could be done."

"I am flattered," said Father John trying not to blush. "I have a second, Father Dominic, who has worked side by side with me since I arrived there. He could easily take over. As it is he who runs the daily classes and does all the arranging and scheduling, often writing letters for me when I am working on other things."

"Then make it so. Go pack up your books and things and come back in two days after you inform the monks of the change. I will have it officially pronounced tomorrow that you are to assume the job of secretary to the Pope."

The Pope was tired so Father John made his leave. Walking back to Saint Martin, the elation she felt was tremendous. This was better than anything imagined, for she would be the Pope's confidant and advisor. She knew the politics surrounding the Pope was prescient, but she was knowledgeable in the art of intrigue and suspicion, and disguise, so courage boosted her steps.

Father John called Dominic into the office when she returned and he was told of the change to be ordered by the Pope.

"No one here wants you to leave. What of the work we have done? It must continue," he said.

"Yes. The Pope is appointing you to take over. The order will come tomorrow. I will be there, not far away, in case you need advice, but please know that I have the utmost confidence that you can handle this. I would not go if I thought this was not the case. Congratulations, Dominic." Father John stood and patted him on the back.

All the next day, the monks filed into the office to wish Father John well and to say that they would miss his guidance. "Be proud of your accomplishments with this community," he told them after dinner. "You have made much progress, but until everyone of our flock is literate and every boy and girl has opportunities for learning and growing, your work must continue."

All the monks stood, and as they left the dining hall, they bowed to Father John in turn.

The next morning, Father John, followed by porters carrying books, made his way to the walled community that housed the head of the Church.

Chapter Thirty

Father John, in becoming the Pope's private secretary, did so at the dismay of others who aspired to that position. Why were they not the favorite of Leo? Had they not served him dutifully in the past? Hearing the rumblings, and realizing that there must be allies even when there is no ulterior motive, Father John rallied the support of all those endeared to him during the past two years in Rome. With no relatives, concubines, or ties anywhere, it became easier to appease the critics and serve the needs of those who came to him, thus creating a loyal following.

Realizing that there also needed to be peace among others also serving the Pope and running the household, he amicably heard the requests of all those who brought issues to be resolved. The atmosphere slowly changed to be more favorable to Father John and the manner in which he intervened for them.

After prayer in the evening, it was not uncommon for Father John to change his garb and become a female in a cloak and take a path underground to an outside door and walk the streets of Rome. She took different paths to explore the city and browse the markets and speak to the people, men and women. No one recognized her, and no one was reticent to speak to the lone woman in the streets. She would often buy fruit and bread and eat as she strolled.

I miss sharing this experience with someone, as Henricus and I did in Athens and before. She had not thought about him in a very long time, not since she left him in the cave as he lay dying. *I also miss the physical comfort we had with each other. Is that forever lost to me? Am I not still a woman with needs and desires?*

She must have looked very pensive that night as she was walking past a man selling leather goods. "Miss, would you like to look at my wares? I am a master leatherworker and have thongs and other items that could interest you."

Picking up a sandal, she noticed the fine craftsmanship of the item and asked, "Do you have one that would fit me?"

"May I see your foot? Perhaps then I can determine what would fit you." He was staring at her fine features and light colored hair that was only partially covered by the cloaked hood.

She lifted the hem of her cloak, careful to hide her monk's undergarment, moving her foot this way and that so he could assess her size.

"Yes, try this one. I think you will find it suits you."

She struggled to put the sandals on and tie the laces while standing so he invited her to sit on his stool. "May I?" he asked as he reached forward to strap the sandals onto her feet.

Not able to keep from blushing at his touch, he finished and looked up at her, noticing the flush on her cheeks.

Quickly she stood and said, "Yes, that is very good. I will take them." Paying quickly, she hurried away, looking back once to see him standing, arms on hips, watching her go.

A few nights later, she again found her way to the market and the leatherworker was there. "You again? Have you worn the sandals out already?"

They both laughed. "No, I am just out for my evening walk and found my way back here. The bread maker is wonderful, and I ate little all day; I was so busy."

"And what is it you work at sweet lady?"

Chapter Thirty

"Oh." On the spot she dreamed up a story. "I am literate. My father was a priest. So I scribe for a host of writers here in Rome. I had a manuscript I had to finish today so I worked through meals."

The leatherworker covered his wares with muslin and shuttered his stall, then walked in front of the stall and motioned for her to follow him. Without hesitation, she did.

"Where are we going?" she asked.

"You will see." They stopped at a food stall that had tables and he brought over a barrel for her to sit on. He disappeared to talk to the proprietor and dragged a second barrel over to sit near.

They were brought wine and cheese, fruit and bread, and dried meats on a platter.

"My name is Agapitus. What is yours?"

"Really?" she smiled. "Beloved. Your parents named you that?"

He laughed. "Yes. They were older when my mother gave birth and were very grateful to have me. Theirs was a love match, both widow and widower. So they called me Agapitus. Yours?"

"Gilberta."

"Are you married, Gilberta?"

"Are you?"

"No. I am waiting for the right person. I want a love match, not one of convenience."

"I am not either."

The two talked and ate and drank for some time. When they finished, she stood and said, "I must make my way back. It is late and I start my work early in the morning. I thank you for the meal and the conversation."

"Come again," he said seriously, taking her hand in his.

"I will try," she answered.

She walked quickly back to the entrance of the residence smiling and thinking to herself, *I want to see him again. I will have to arrange more evening walks after the Pope retires.* So she did. They talked and shared the evening, and one night rather than stopping to eat, he steered her to his home and they made love. She would return as often as she could, she told him.

Knowing the wants and needs of the Pope, she served him dutifully, taking on more and more responsibility. But Leo was getting old and his rheumatism had all but disabled him. Not even Father John could allay the pain for long, as Leo's overall health deteriorated.

Finally, the fitful, failing Pope was moved in a black litter by four monks to an underground church and placed in front of an altar while incense burned, physicians attended, and psalms were sung to stave off the inevitable. This lion of a Pope who built fortifications around Rome, amassed treasures, staved off the Saracens, beautified churches, and made the papacy more powerful was reduced by age and illness.

For three days he lingered in pain, motionless, without eating or drinking. Not even Father John's powerful teas would he allow to pass his lips. Finally, he breathed his last and was declared deceased.

Leo's body was anointed, washed with oil and wine, cloaked in the finest robe, and carried to its final service in the Church of St. Peter, then buried in holy ground.

The mourners turned out in the piazza of St. Peter, all speculating on the line of succession for the next Pope. At midday, as was the custom in the year 855, Popes were selected in the marketplace, with wine flowing and blood spurting from vying factions who all wanted power and fought with sticks and stones. Votes were promised with wine and gold, and women traded kisses in the forum for support of their candidate. They traded their one guaranteed possession, their vote, for favors for their candidate.

Chapter Thirty

Father John, standing on the terrace of Saint Martin, hands crossed across his chest, stood in wait, long ago having coalesced his supporters for his ambitious desires. They were numerous; he had four hundred pupils, monks of his order, and courtiers who had received favors from him. His beauty garnished the vote of women, and Leo's servants supported him as well; they went out to obtain support from the people and promised that a Pope with no nephews or favors to others would spread the wealth of St. Peter to the poor.

For four full hours, Father John grew pale and flushed in turn as the tide of the voters went one way, then another. Falling into a marble seat slowly, he heard the shouting as the people approached Saint Martin.

"Hail to the new Pope, John VIII. Hail to the victor, our new learned Pope."

Mounting the stairs, someone placed the purple robe around Father John's shoulders, removed the sandals made by the leather-worker, and placed the slippers with the cross on his feet. Descending the steps, the shoes fell off at least three times because they were too large for a woman's foot.

At the base of Saint Martin, a mule awaited to take the new Pope from Saint John the Lateran, the headquarters of Christianity, to San Clemente, the private church of the Pope. Father John mounted and the mule was led down the street toward the church.

Inside, the triple diadem was placed on the head of Father John, the symbol of sovereignty over Rome, the world, and heaven. Scribes wrote the formal results of the election as the crowds outside were noisy in acclamation of their new spiritual and secular leader.

While this was occurring, hearing of his brother Leo's illness, the King of England came into the church, went up to John, and kissed his feet, rendering his estate tributary to the Holy See. Ambassadors arrived from Constantinople bringing presents for the new Pope.

Overcome with joy at achieving her ambitions, Pope John stood, arms raised to heaven, and proclaimed to all, "I thank thee," repeating the phrase over and over, misty eyed from his success. "I thank thee."

chapter Thirty-one

At almost forty years old, Pope John was experienced and learned, and he defended and sustained his predecessor's traditions. All spiritual and worldly matters were dealt with fairly and evenly, and during this time, he appeared drunk with power as he ordained bishops, built churches, and even crowned Lothair's successor, Louis, as sole emperor of Italy.

After achieving all you desire, what is left to do with your life, he thought deeply as he entered the second year of his reign. *I am at a loss to see a crossroad to decide which way to travel. All roads lead back here. I have become more than I ever dreamed as a poor child who was run out of her home by a stepmother in Mainz. Everything I have learned came to bear in this position, and I believe I am ruling wisely and fairly. Yet, what of the need to advance further. To be more, that force has driven my life and ambitions. Once achieved, what is left?*

Yet, there was an undercurrent of dissatisfaction among those that thought they would benefit directly from Leo's treasure. That was impossible considering the amount that the Pope spent on other matters, including banquets and feasts for visiting dignitaries paying tribute to the Pope. What was ignored was more accumulation of wealth, and that without lands to pillage and wars to be won, the only way to replenish the coffers was from the people of Rome. That was not something Father John wanted to do.

I am surrounded by a circle of vultures, all waiting their turn to ravish the spoils, thought John, fairly early into the reign. *I should go out to the streets again and speak to the people and hear their grumblings.*

To leave the residence as the Pope's secretary was one thing. To leave as Pope was another entirely. The aide slept just outside her chamber to be at the ready for any whim the Pope had during the night. *I will have to sneak out without him knowing. Perhaps an herbal sleep aid will deepen his dreams.*

Delving into her cases there was a formulary. The next night, a brew awaited the aide by his bedside. Pope John visited and said, "Something to ward off the cough going around. Drink it before you fall asleep while it is hot. I already took mine."

"Thank you. I will."

Watching him empty the cup, she removed it and returned to her room. Changing into a simple cloak and the sandals the leatherworker made for her, she went down a back staircase, remaining out of sight, and out into the streets of Rome once again. She was Gilberta again for the evening; she walked the streets and went to the market where the leatherworker plied his wares. He was not there. Asking other merchants, "Where is the leatherworker? I left a pair of shoes with him and wanted to pick them up."

"He had to travel to Ostia to meet a boat to get more leather coming off a ship. He should be back in a few days," a kind woman who sold fish informed her.

"I see." Gilberta thought this was a chance to talk to the people and see what they thought of Pope John.

"How is your business, kind woman?"

"All right. Could be better if the people had more money in their pockets. Instead they buy heads, tails, and fins before they buy the meat of the fish."

"Do they have less now than before?"

Chapter Thirty-One

"Yes and no. They are just more cautious."

"Cautious about what? People earn money, and they have food to eat."

"Yes, but they did not work very hard for a while after Pope John was crowned. We thought we would share in the wealth. That did not happen. Now, most are short of funds."

A bread maker nearby joined in the conversation. "Yes. We got him the votes, but no promises were kept."

"Were promises given?" asked Gilberta.

"He is an outsider. Everyone knows that you repay people for their vote. I guess no one told the Pope that. You do something to make their lives better. Instead people are tightening their belts because there is less money around. Meanwhile, there are big building projects and more and more bishops to be fed and clothed, and the people are ignored."

A small crowd of vendors gathered and joined in the conversation, and Gilberta realized for the first time that the population had to be appeased before lofty goals were achieved, especially in a time of peace. When there was a war, everyone understood sacrifices had to be made, but when there was relative peace, the people demanded their due.

She walked on and spoke to different groups of people, all speaking about the same things, and her heart softened to their plight. She would figure out a solution and return as soon as she could.

Sneaking back to the palace, Pope John changed clothes, looked in on the sleeping aid, and lay down to rest.

The aide, having had an unusually long sleep, woke the Pope at about ten in the morning. Pope John washed, dressed, and went to contemplate the plight of the people and what he could do to aid them.

He sat pensively for a long time, softened in his heart for the people the Pope owed gratitude to and should protect. Finally, an idea surfaced, and his secretary was called in.

"I would like to look over the accounts of the papacy since I came to aid Pope Leo. I want an accounting of the expenses and income to assess where the coffers are lacking in sufficient income. We have churches all around and perhaps the outflow to them should not exceed the income to us so that we may help those around us more. Do this swiftly, please."

By the next day, Pope John had pored over all the books and decided that the tithe paid to the papacy by the churches it supported was too low and that all such institutions should increase their contributions by 5 percent, effective immediately.

"Here is my decision, signed. I need you to witness this and transmit it to all that it requires. Then I want to initiate a direct way to receive their tithe because I see that many are in arrears. Take care of this and appoint some men to collect in an orderly manner and without malice. If someone cannot pay now, work out a payment schedule," he told his secretary.

"Yes, your Holiness," the secretary responded.

"Here is another paper. I want some men to go out into the populace and talk to them of their expectations of the papacy. What do they want from us and how can we ease their lives? Report back to me in a few days."

Feeling very good about his actions, Father John once again transformed himself into Gilberta, gave the aide a strong brew to ensure sleep, and went out into the evening.

The leatherworker was back. Gilberta walked over to him, and he immediately closed his stall, leading her to his rooms where they spent most of the night. Before dawn, she dressed.

"I hope this does not lead to a child," he told her.

Chapter Thirty-One

"I am over forty years old and have already started the end of that time of month, so I am sure that could not happen. I have never been very fertile," she said as she leaned over the straw mattress to kiss him.

"Why can't you stay with me for the whole night?"

"You know I have work to do. I will return when I can. When I am done with the work I am currently immersed in."

Within a month, all the changes Pope John put in place had an effect on the coffers of the papacy. With this new found source of funds, he pored over the wants of the people compiled by the secretary. Prioritizing them, he created a system of aid for the people based on need, and made arrangements for regular disbursements for which the people had to send a household member, preferably the wife, to collect.

Nearing the end of the second year of his reign, the people were appeased and the tithe to the churches and abbeys were just a part of life for the support of the papacy. All was going so well that Gilberta found time to regularly venture to the marketplace, often showing up at closing time to meet with her leatherworker. The complaints of the merchants in the marketplace turned to praise for the Pope. She smiled as she passed the fish seller bartering with a customer for the flesh of a fish.

When he had reached the pinnacle of his desires and attained the highest accolades possible, Pope John became bolder and more reckless, sneaking out more often, meeting more than twice a week with her lover, walking freely through the streets of Rome, and orderly conducting and mediating all wants and needs of the demands of the position he held.

In the twentieth month of the papacy, Gilberta noticed that her time of the month, which had been more than sporadic her whole life, had finally ceased, and she was free of having to hide the bloody rags under her papal robes from those who tried to dress and undress her. A sense of satisfaction spread over her, one that she had never really known, one of peace with who she was. Her need for more accolades was finally abated and contentment with her life and position was hers.

Chapter Thirty-Two

The Pope, in reality a middle-aged woman with little experience or knowledge about the vagaries of the female body, having lived with men since the age of twelve, easily accepted her growing girth and placed blame on the rich food served at feasts and dinners within the papal residency. Her leatherworker, whom she met regularly in the evening, remarked on her figure, but both felt that at forty-two and middle-aged, they were free of the worries of pregnancy, and he enjoyed her added girth.

One evening, in his bed, Father John felt the first flurries of movement in his belly, but ascribed it to the food and drink of the evening fare. There had been a feast for visiting dignitaries the night before. He rolled over and fell back to sleep, having matters of import to deal with the next day.

Failing crops and a plague of locusts having beset the region, the Pope decided that he needed to pray at the Lateran church and organized a procession for the next week to allay the fears of the people that the papacy was doing something to change their luck and save the fields that fed the insects. As swiftly as they arrived, a cold spell and high wind carried the locusts off, saving at least half the crops from devastation.

"Let us arrange a prayer vigil at the Lateran church for next week. Let the people know that the Pope will go there to invoke thanks to the Lord for saving the fields from further destruction and we welcome those who want to join the Pope along the way," he said to his aide.

On the appointed day, Father John was in great discomfort. Pains in his belly were coming in waves, and his stomach and bowels had emptied themselves of the contents of the evening meal repeatedly during the night.

Gray and ashen the morning of the event, the aide asked, "Are you well, your Holiness? You do not look like you can withstand the procession? Shall we postpone it?"

"Definitely not. It was just something I ate. I will take some herbs and quiet my stomach before we leave. No rich food for me anymore. I have learned my lesson. I fared better when the food was simple and less abundant. Could you please see to that from now on?"

"As you wish."

After serving the Lord and the people of Rome for two years and five months, the Pope dressed himself with some effort and drank an herbal tea to calm the pain in his stomach. As was the custom, the route was followed through the streets with crowds of people cheering the Pope and following him along the way.

Father John, with waves of great discomfort plaguing him, waved as he rode the mule and smiled as best as he could at the people, blessing the throngs as he went. Nearing the Coliseum, the procession turned down toward the Lateran and proceeded along the street. Halfway down the most direct route to San Clemente, Father John felt faint with pain and fell off the mule onto the ground. Immediately surrounded by the procession, he held his stomach tightly, eyes shut with the pain, calling out, "Help me, help me."

Those in attendance saw steaks of red emerge from under the robes and trickle down the stones in the street. Lifting the robes,

Chapter Thirty-Two

they found a male baby being delivered on the spot, umbilical cord still attached to the Pope.

Bleeding profusely, Pope John fell in and out of consciousness as they lifted the male child from the folds of the papal finery, now soaked with red. The baby died shortly after and Gilberta's bleeding did not abate, even with the expulsion of the afterbirth.

The realization that they had been seduced by Father John, now Pope John VIII, and that in fact he was a woman, froze those in papal attendance into inaction. They stood there in disbelief and could find no course of action as this was so alien to their rituals and way of thinking about the Pope.

The throng of people nearby became aware of the source of the consternation, and started to yell out, "This is the devil's work. Who took over the body of Pope John? What is this witchcraft we are witnessing?" Ignorant and unable to grasp the charade perpetrated on them, they took matters into their own hands in the way they eliminated all they could not explain. They picked up stones and sticks from the road and started to pelt the charlatan repeatedly. Gilberta opened her eyes and saw the onslaught. In the last moments of her life, she saw herself as a child in Mainz, determined to do whatever was needed to study and escape the oppression of the system of rules that would not allow it. She remembered the two loves of her life, Henricus and her leatherworker. She thought of her mentors, Rabinus in Fulda, her teachers in Athens, and of course dear Leo who mentored her and brought her to Rome. Content that she had achieved all her goals and that her life had fulfilled her every expectation, she closed her eyes. What little life still clung to by Gilberta was stoned out of her. Her life had finally ended.

The crowd fell back after this. The bishops and aides, not knowing what else to do, decided to bury the body right there along with her baby. No papal finery, no ritual, and no honoring. They felt duped by Father John, duped into going against all that they expected from a male Pope. They were tricked for so many years into thinking this person was male. Gone in an instant was all the accomplishments and wise counsel delivered by a remarkable person who guided them and won the trust of their beloved Leo. Instead, they sought to preserve the tradition and dignity of the papacy and bury their mistake forever. They turned their backs to the most learned one who aided them and provided spiritual support. They would subsequently hide all mention in their writings of the twenty-nine months and four days of the papacy of Pope John.

They hurried back to the papal residence and cleaned out Pope John's private rooms. Along the wall of the back of the bed was found a bag full of the clothes that Gilberta wore when she left in the night. All was burned and scrubbed to prepare for the next Pope.

Nicholas I was chosen swiftly by the people of Rome. His procession for coronation was a problem that the bishops brought up to be resolved.

"We cannot go down the Lateran to San Clemente any more. No one will soon forget the abomination that transpired there. We must help them forget. There must be an alternative route mapped out, even if it means we have to travel farther."

"Yes, the Vicus Papissa, street of the woman Pope, must forever be bypassed. We must erase her from the annuls and change traditions to rid her from memory," Nicholas added.

"We must ensure this can never happen again," said one of the bishops.

"Ensure this will never happen again? How can we?" asked another.

Chapter Thirty-Two

"By ensuring maleness. By checking the elected pontiff before coronation," said Nicolas.

The bishops looked at each other in wonder, until one said, "We could ask for proof. We could devise a way to physically ensure maleness. A chair perhaps with an open bottom, like a birthing chair, a *sedia stercoraria*, where he sat fully clad and someone could reach underneath and feel for male organs."

They all looked at each other and nodded in agreement. Thus, a ritual was devised whereby the gender of subsequent Popes would be insured.

The papacy continued, but on the Vicus Papissa, on the spot where she died, was erected a small statue of the Pope holding a baby. Inscribed on the makeshift tombstone were the words *Parce, Papter Patrum, Papisse, Prodere, Partum* (forbear, father of fathers, to betray the child bearing of the female Pope).

The papacy could not afford the scandal of elevating a woman to the papacy. The kinglike manner of the Pope in the ninth century needed to be preserved for there to be power and order in the Church. Scandal was out of the question if Rome was to maintain its semblance of control and reach. Systematically, all the documentation about Pope John was hidden in the archives of the Church, accessible to no outsider. No one spoke or wrote about any of his accomplishments. No one spoke his name and the line of succession remained a blank page with Leo followed by Nicholas.

In spite of this, rumors persisted and the people told tales of the remarkable learned Pope, the fair haired child who came from humble beginnings and did what she had to do in order to study and survive in a world that was barred from females. They talked of her journey from Mainz to Fulda, from Fulda to Athens, and Athens to Rome. She would serve forever as a model for other girls who wanted more than short lives of toiling and serving others, cleaning and sewing, barely learning to read and write their names. They too would dream of having a different life, a life equal in opportunity to men, rather than being stifled and snuffed out by custom and tradition.

The information in this book is loosely based on:

Emmanuel J. Rhodes, *Pope Joan, An Historical Romance*, trans. J. H. Freese, M.A. (London: H. J. Cook, 1800), https://books.google.com/books/reader?id=rwk7AQAAMAAJ&printsec=frontcover&output=reader&pg=GBS.

www.ingramcontent.com/pod-product-compliance
Lightning Source LLC
Chambersburg PA
CBHW051358290426
44108CB00015B/2066